A
SACRED
SORROW

EXPERIENCE GUIDE

A

SACRED

SORROW

EXPERIENCE GUIDE

A
SACRED
SORROW

REACHING OUT TO GOD IN
THE LOST LANGUAGE OF LAMENT

EXPERIENCE GUIDE

✦

MICHAEL CARD

NAVPRESS

Discipleship Inside Out™

NAVPRESS
Discipleship Inside Out™

NavPress is the publishing ministry of The Navigators, an international Christian organization and leader in personal spiritual development. NavPress is committed to helping people grow spiritually and enjoy lives of meaning and hope through personal and group resources that are biblically rooted, culturally relevant, and highly practical.

For a free catalog go to www.NavPress.com
or call 1.800.366.7788 in the United States or 1.800.839.4769 in Canada.

ISBN-13: 978-1-57683-668-2

Cover design: studiogearbox.com
Cover image: Getty/Adalberto Rios Lanz/Sexto Sol
Creative Team: Rachelle Gardner, Darla Hightower, Arvid Wallen, Glynese Northam

Unless otherwise identified, all Scripture quotations in this publication are taken from the HOLY BIBLE: NEW INTERNATIONAL VERSION® (NIV®). Copyright © 1973, 1978, 1984 by International Bible Society. Used by permission of Zondervan Publishing House. All rights reserved. Other versions used include: The Jewish Publication Society Bible (JPS), copyright © 1985 by The Jewish Publication Society.

Printed in the United States of America

4 5 6 7 8 9 10 11 / 14 13 12 11 10

CONTENTS

FOREWORD   9

WEEK ONE

VOCABULARY AND CONCEPTS   13
   DAY 1: Wilderness "Worth-ship"   16
   DAY 2: Presence   20
   DAY 3: Hesed   23
   DAY 4: Formula of Remembrance   26
   DAY 5: Vav Adversative   29

WEEK TWO

JOB: A FRUSTRATED LAMENTER   33
   DAY 1: The Story: Job 1:1–2:10   35
   DAY 2: Three Friends: Job 2:11-13   36
   DAY 3: First Lament: Job 3   37
   DAY 4: Second and Third Lament: Job 6:1–7:21; 10:1-22   38
   DAY 5: Speaking the Language of Lament for Yourself   39

WEEK THREE

JOB: THE COMPLETION OF THE EQUATION   41
   DAY 1: Fourth Lament: Job 13:17–14:22   42
   DAY 2: Fifth Lament: Job 29:1–31:40   43
   DAY 3: The Divine Questions: Job 38:1–40:2; 42:7-9   44
   DAY 4: The Costly Vision: Job 9:33-35; 16:19-21; 19:25-27   45
   DAY 5: Speaking the Language of Lament for Yourself   47

Week Four

David: A Life Fashioned for Lament   49
   Day 1: A Future King: 1 Samuel 16   51
   Day 2: A Lament for an Enemy and a Friend: 2 Samuel 1   52
   Day 3: A Lament Beyond Words: 2 Samuel 18   53
   Day 4: A Brief Introduction to David's Lament Psalms   55
   Day 5: Speaking the Language of Lament for Yourself   57

Week Five

David: Composer of Lament   59
   Day 1: "How Long?": Psalm 13   60
   Day 2: A Lament of Repentance: Psalm 51; 2 Samuel 11–12 61
   Day 3: From Confidence to Doubt: Psalm 27   62
   Day 4: "Why?": Psalm 22   63
   Day 5: Speaking the Language of Lament for Yourself   65

Week Six

Jeremiah: A Difficult Hope   67
   Day 1: A Costly Call: Jeremiah 1   69
   Day 2: A Cruel King: Jeremiah 36   70
   Day 3: The Cost of the Call: Jeremiah 37–38; 40:1–6   72
   Day 4: A Nightmare Come True: Jeremiah 39; 52   73
   Day 5   Speaking the Language of Lament for Yourself   74

Week Seven

The Lamentations of Jeremiah: The View from a Cave   77
   Day 1: A Lonely, Weeping Widow: Lamentations 1   79
   Day 2: When God Is Your Enemy: Lamentations 2   80
   Day 3: The Pain Becomes Personal: Lamentations 3   81
   Day 4: A Supremely Sickening Vision: Lamentations 4–5   83
   Day 5: Speaking the Language of Lament for Yourself   84

WEEK EIGHT

JESUS: ALL THINGS COME TOGETHER   87
   DAY 1: *Hesed* Infleshed: John 1:1-14   89
   DAY 2: Enemy Love: Luke 6:27-36   91
   DAY 3: Another Weeping Prophet: Luke 13:34-35; 19:41-44 92
   DAY 4: Lament and the Meal: Luke 22:14-38; John 13   94
   DAY 5 Speaking the Language of Lament for Yourself   95

WEEK NINE

JESUS: THE MAN OF SORROWS   97
   DAY 1: Crossing the Line in the Garden: Luke 22:39-46   98
   DAY 2: The God-Forsaken God: Matthew 27:45-46   99
   DAY 3: Job's Vision Realized   100
   DAY 4: The Voice of David's Lament   102
   DAY 5: Speaking the Language of Lament for Yourself   103

WEEK TEN

CONCLUSIONS   105
   DAY 1: The Key to Renewed Presence: Genesis 3   106
   DAY 2: The Sweet Scroll: Ezekiel 2:9-3:3   108
   DAY 3: Lamenting the Thorns: 2 Corinthians 12:7-10   109
   DAY 4: The End of Lament: Revelation 7:17; 21:3-5   110
   DAY 5: Looking Back to See How Far We've Come   112

ANNOTATED BIBLIOGRAPHY   115

AUTHOR   121

THE PATH

BY KEN COPE

Over the twenty-five years that I have been involved in ministry, counseling, and coaching, I have worked with many hurting people who are struggling to understand themselves and to understand God. One of the main issues that has continued to surface in my work has to do with unresolved loss. We are taught that grieving is feeling sorry for yourself, and that real strength is to not show any emotion at all. Because we do not know how to be sad, we want to get to the end-stage of grief; we want the benefits and the results of healing, but we do not want to take the time to move through the often long and painful process of grief. For too long we have been taught that shedding tears is a sign of weakness and that you must not wallow in your sorrow. And the mandate of Psalm 46:10, "be still, and know that I am God," is lost.

As a result of this approach to grief, we have a whole generation of people with unresolved issues, hurts, and pains in their past that have been shallowly dealt with at best, and at worst have been ignored and discounted completely. The result has been an increasingly shallow Christianity and a profound lack of understanding of the nature of God and how, as His people, we are to move and live in a fallen world. We do not know ourselves. And while we know a lot *about* God, we do not truly know Him. We have been unwilling to sit in our sadness and pain, and we have missed much of the intimacy that He longs to offer us.

My experience with lament and with the living God occurred several years ago, when I was diagnosed with a degenerative liver disease. My father had died when I was seventeen, and now faced with the possibility that I might die, leaving behind my seventeen-year-old son and fourteen-year-old daughter, I was overwhelmed with feelings of anger and confusion and pain. When I finally let go and cried out to God, it was in fury and frustration that I unleashed on Him, accusing Him, questioning Him. It did not make any sense to me. How could a loving God allow my children to go through the pain that I had? I had done all that He had asked of me. I had been a faithful servant and made the right choices and sacrifices. Why was He doing this to me? How dare He? I was certain that I had pushed Him too far, that I was now going to experience His wrath and condemnation for my ranting and unbelief. But what I found instead was great mercy and tenderness. I experienced His loving-kindness in a way that I never had before. He had been waiting all along for me to come to the end of myself and fall on my knees before Him. He had been waiting for me to be completely honest with who I was, instead of who I thought I should be. And I realized that it was in my brokenness and weakness that I was truly able to know the tremendous love that my great God has for me. He could take anything that I hurled at Him. He was not going to let me go.

Several years ago a well-known Christian artist found his way into my office. After spending several hours talking over his concerns, I realized that he really didn't know who he was, and over the years of ministry he had grown out of touch with the core of who God made him to be. After several hours of talking and probing into his history and the nature of his relationship with his parents, I said to him, "You know, a lot of what you are doing with your audiences and with your wife are the same things you did as a child. You are still that little boy, sliding pictures and poking your fingers underneath the door of your dad's study, trying to get the attention and involvement from him that he so generously gave to his patients during the day."

When the reality of what I had said hit him, he broke down and sobbed in a way that I've only heard one other time, when I was attending an African funeral in a village in the bush. As I approached this funeral, I could hear the people wailing from a great distance, long before I had reached the village. Fortunately for Africans, they have not been taught to hide their emotions. Their deep, soulish sobs, as well as the ones of this Christian artist, were tears of pain from the deepest well of the soul.

That artist was Michael Card. That day I suggested to Mike that he might want to use his own language of music to probe deeper into the unresolved issues with his earthly father. Out of this came a song called "Underneath the Door." Since that experience years ago, Mike has persisted in digging into the depths of his heart and soul, working through unresolved issues and losses and pains in his past and his present. Being the faithful scholar that he is, Mike has searched the Scriptures to find the purpose of grief and lament, which are gifts God has given us to know better how to survive and grow and live in an imperfect world.

As Mike has worked through his issues with his past, as well as relationships in the present, he has become a richer, deeper, and more loving individual. He has become more open and vulnerable, and he is able to connect with his family and friends in a more meaningful and deeper way. Now I not only get to see the image of God come through his music and his writings, but I also get to experience the person of Jesus Christ through Mike's spirit and his presence.

I believe that you will be blessed as you work through this experience guide of lament, because the heart of Mike's message does not come from dry theology or theory. It comes from a man who has truly surrendered himself at the foot of the cross and who has been willing to wait in the wilderness and say to his heavenly Father, *not my will but Thine*. What you'll read and experience in these pages is the journey of a man who is pursuing the heart of God.

We live in a fallen world, full of disappointment and loss, and we often feel empty and unfulfilled and incredibly alone. But while God is not there to fix our problems and make the pain go away, He is always walking beside us. In the ongoing journey of life, we are given the opportunity to know Him and ourselves through the process of lamenting and grieving. Our traditional view of grief is that it should be reserved for funerals and tragedies. However, if we really want to encounter God and grow in our relationship with Him, then our attitude toward grief must change from viewing it as an uncomfortable and unwanted drop-in visitor to seeing it as a dear and faithful companion that is an integral part of our daily journey with God. It is there to allow us to enter into the heart of Philippians 3:10, which is an invitation to share in the fellowship of His suffering. When we allow ourselves to feel broken and alone, we gain a small measure of understanding of the sacrifice that Christ made for us in going to the cross and being broken for us. Grief draws us to God Himself in ways that could not be accomplished through any other means. My prayer is that as you embark on this journey of understanding the role of lament in your own life that you will find a greater and deeper intimacy with Christ and a more humble confidence to face each day.

VOCABULARY AND CONCEPTS

INTRODUCTION

Before you, a narrow pathway extends into a dark terrain. Perhaps you have crossed it at various times in your life, maybe even traveled for a season within its boundaries. The path is lament, and this study will help you explore its length more deliberately.

The Bible promises that the path is going *somewhere*. Though it frequently passes through the "valley of the shadow of death," that is not its final end.

First, there are a few milestones, signposts, with which we must become familiar. Our first week will be spent learning to read them and follow their direction along the way. But more than direction, they will give a sense of shape and meaning to what can sometimes appear to be a senseless and confusing journey. Perhaps you might even consider them lampposts like the one on the border of Narnia, marking the boundary between one land and another completely different one.

Once the trek begins, we will be joined by other, infinitely more experienced travelers. We will meet the first—Job—and walk with him for a time. We will follow in his footsteps in order to gain our direction and learn the proper pace. Without his help in the beginning of the trip, we would most likely lose our way.

Next, we will take up with David. Having begun to get accustomed to the landscape, our time with him will provide us with priceless and hard-fought knowledge of how to deal with all the various terrain. The road may turn sharply uphill or might skirt a precipice. The landscape will, no doubt, be dark. David will enable us to follow the path no matter how steep, rocky, or threatening.

Just as we part company with David, Jeremiah will join us. He will teach us how to follow the course with a crowd, as well as when we are utterly alone. He, perhaps as no one we've met thus far, has fallen more often along this path of lament. His knees are more bruised and bloody. He will understand if we long to turn back and look for home. He will remind us that our final home lies at the other end of the trail, in the direction we are already heading. Most importantly, Jeremiah will prepare us, will teach us to recognize the most important Guide we will encounter along the path of lament.

Finally, at what seems the far end of the trail, we will encounter Jesus. We will find Him waiting for us. In His company we will discover that what we thought was the end is, in fact, the beginning. What felt like the last of our strength has become the first. The trail will become no less rough or steep with Him, yet we will find it a different trail.

If you are ready, let's begin. I would like to be able to tell you that it will be easy, but it will not. In fact, these next ten weeks might be the most spiritually strenuous in your life. But I am as certain as faith can make one certain that we are, you and I, called to follow this path wherever it goes. And it promises to go someplace wonderful.

WHAT IS A LAMENT?

Lament is not a word we typically use in everyday conversation. What does it mean? Is it simply a sad song?

Biblical laments are "songs"—that is, they are made up of lyrics. When you look at the way they are set aside in the margins of your Bible, you can tell they're poetic in structure. Most of them were originally set to music. Many have musical notations, naming a well-known melody, or perhaps describing what kinds of instruments they were written for. Look at Psalm 22, one of the most poignant laments in the Bible. It was to be played to the tune of a long lost melody entitled, "The Doe of the Morning." The musical notes for the laments in Habakkuk occur at the very end; "For the director of music. On my stringed instruments (3:19)." David, who composed most of the laments in the Bible, was a fine harpist (see 1 Samuel 16:16-23) but also composed for flutes (for example, Psalm 5 superscription) and other "stringed instruments" (see Psalm 4 superscription). Psalm 81 lists other musical instruments like the tambourine, lyre, and ram's horn. So clearly the Bible indicates that laments are at least lyrical, if not almost certainly song lyrics.

But are laments always sad? Many of them are poignant, such as David's lament for his friend Jonathan in 2 Samuel 1:19-27. But others are filled with fear (Psalm 55:5), confusion (Psalm 13), or even the blackest hatred (Psalm 109). In fact, the full range of human emotions is to be found in the laments of the Bible.

HOW IS THIS STUDY ORGANIZED?

This is a ten-week study. Each week has an introduction and then is divided into five days of study. Each week will involve reading, both in this book and in the Bible. There will also be questions on which to reflect and discuss and opportunities for journaling. Finally, you will have the chance to begin writing your own laments. This is called an "Experience Guide" because the central purpose is for you to experience a new and deeper type of interaction with God—biblical lament.

LECTIO DIVINA

As you work through the various Scripture readings, you might try using an ancient form called the *lectio divina* or "divine reading." This is a simple method which involves reading through a passage of Scripture three times. The first time, called the *lectio,* you simply let the words wash over you, never straining to "solve the puzzle." Initially you listen to the words of Scripture with the "ears of your heart." When you are finished with this first reading, spend some quiet time listening to what you remember about the text. This is called the *meditatio,* or meditation.

The second time, as you read, ask the Holy Spirit to speak directly to your heart through some phrase or word in the text. This is called the *oratio.* Finally, spend some time savoring this word as a precious gift. Again, do not strain to decipher it; only receive it as a gift.

On your final read through, move slowly once more through the entire passage. When you come to the special verse that was the Spirit's gift to you, pause one final moment and listen to it with a heart of thanksgiving. Allow yourself to rest in the given-ness of God's Word to you. This is called the *contemplatio.*

This ancient method of reading the Bible is more about connecting with God and less about straining to achieve a didactic understanding of the text. It relies on the simple belief that, alone with the Scripture before God, anyone who is willing to come can receive the Word as a priceless gift.

(I am thankful to Bob and Claudia Mitchell for teaching me this ancient technique during a Navigators retreat at Glen Eyrie.)

WILDERNESS "WORTH-SHIP"

When Isaiah and later John cried out their message of preparing a way and making it straight, they made clear where this "way" would be experienced: *in the wilderness.* It is only in the desert places that we pick up the trail of lament.

ISRAEL

> The LORD, the God of the Hebrews, sent me to say, "Let My
> people go that they may *worship Me in the wilderness.*"
> (Exodus 7:16, JPS)[1]

These were the final words of God through Moses before the plagues were to descend upon Egypt. God's intention was deliverance for His people and *the goal of deliverance is always worship.*

The purpose of their hard-won freedom was not simply emancipation. The purpose was the worship of God. And notice the place where their worship was to begin: "in the wilderness." True worship always begins in the wilderness.

In the wilderness, the children of Israel discovered God's worth. When they were thirsty, the rock would be struck and water miraculously provided (see Exodus 16; Numbers 20; 1 Corinthians 10:4). When they were attacked, God told the people, "Stand still, I will fight for you" (see Exodus 14:14). The people discovered what their God was worth. In fact, the first primitive form of the word worship was "worth-ship."

Through worship, we offer ourselves to God (see Romans 12:1). Along the pathway of lament we realize that the invitation of Scripture is to offer *all* of our emotional lives to God—our joys as well as our sorrows, the full spectrum of our hearts, including even the hatred we have for our enemies. As the path winds through the desert, we discover the dimensions of thirst and find out that the Rock is still with us, providing living water. When we are hungry, He feeds us with Himself. In the wilderness we discover how much He is worth. This is an uncharted area of worship for most Christians today. We need to rediscover this lost and overgrown path.

---

1. This quote comes from the JPS (Jewish Publication Society), an excellent translation of the Old Testament.

JOB

Remember what Job did when he first entered into the wilderness of his suffering, when he heard that all his children had been killed? He *worshiped* (see 1:20). His worship was in the form of lament, and through it Job offered up to God the deepest disappointment and sorrow of his heart. At the end of his long journey of lament, Job discovered a new depth to the worth of God.

DAVID

When David was lost in the wilderness of his sin with Bathsheba, how did he find his way back? He worshiped (see Psalm 51). His worship was in the form of a lament of contrition, and through it David found that God had been waiting all along to meet him, forgive him, and restore him. David found God waiting there on the pathway of lament.

JEREMIAH

As he stood over the smoldering ruins of Jerusalem and finally witnessed the unthinkable destruction he had prophetically seen for so long, Jeremiah felt within his heart both the sorrow of his seemingly forsaken people, as well as the wordless grief of the God whom they had forsaken. The Holy City had become a deserted wasteland. The only pathway out of the ruins of both the city and the spiritual lives of the people was lament. Jeremiah composed and conducted laments on behalf of both Israel and God.

JESUS

When Jesus was forced to wander through that darkest of death's shadows, the deep blackness of the sin of the world, it was through His cries of lament that He held on to the "joy set before him" (Hebrews 12:2). He was worshiping there on that cross, for there He demonstrated and the world discovered that God alone was worthy. Jesus' worship took on the only form it could have taken: the form of lament. Through it He offered His confusion and desolation to God as an act of worship. And, as Hebrews 5:7 says, "he was heard."

TABERNACLES IN THE WILDERNESS

In the wilderness, Moses had been shown the pattern for the Tabernacle. There the people were to gather to "meet with God." And over it hovered the Presence of the cloud by day and the fire by night. At the center of this big tent complex was the Holy of Holies, where the Ark of the Covenant was placed. Above it resided the Presence.

If Pentecost (see Acts 2) suggests anything to us, it is that we have become God's tabernacles in the wilderness of this fallen world. The flaming tongues of fire that hovered over the heads of those early Christians were the sure sign that God's Spirit had come to inhabit them, even as He had filled the Tabernacle.

We have inside of us something like a Holy of Holies. Its shape is defined by our sorrows, though it is meant to be filled with our joy. Like the inner room of the tabernacle in the wilderness, it is a sacred place that can only be entered by a priest, by our High Priest. He is also known as the Man of Sorrows, who is acquainted with our grief (see Isaiah 53:3). It had been His intention all along to enter into that holiest of places in your life, that place that He already knows so well. It is a wilderness place. It must be so. If you and I are going to meet with Him there, it must be by way of lament.

At a time when so many of us talk about worship, the Scriptures are calling us beyond a shallow experience of good feelings to the place of Job, David, Jeremiah, and Jesus. This is a place where we come to realize that God wants every part of us, everything we have to give, especially our sorrow and pain, for those must become our offerings of biblical worship. The glorious truth is, God wants it all!

Suggested Bible Readings: Exodus 12:31–15:18; Mark 1:1-13

REFLECT & DISCUSS:

1. What parts of yourself have you *not* been offering to God in worship?

2. Can you think of times in your life when your personal "wilderness" led you to worship?

Journal Thought: What is God worth?

(Note: Please don't feel you need to be prolific in the journaling sections. Write what comes to you. A sentence or two is fine—or several pages! This is your own journey. There are no rules.)

PRESENCE

If you listen closely enough to the laments of Scripture you will always hear an echo, like the sound of a voice bounding from the walls of a vast, empty cathedral. That echo is caused by the emptiness that only comes from a perceived absence of God's Presence (rendered with a capital P to indicate it refers to Divine Presence). If you have ever performed musically, you can attest to the fact that this echo can have a beautiful effect on the music. It is the same with the song of our lives, even the songs of lament.

What torments Job most is not his losses, not even the physical pain he experiences, but the fact that God's Presence seems to be absent. In the end Job's troubles are solved not by getting his possessions back, nor the children he lost. In the end, Job gets God back. The hopeless echo of his lament disappears as God comes dangerously and unbelievably close.

"Fill me with joy in your presence," David exults in Psalm 16:11. But there is a darker side to the issue of God's Presence that intersects precisely with lament. This is when God's Presence seems to be impossibly absent. The abject hopelessness of the psalmist echoes throughout the laments:

"Do not cast me from your presence" (Psalm 51:11).

"Why do you hide yourself in times of trouble?" (Psalm 10:1).

"God has forgotten; he covers his face and never sees" (Psalm 10:11).

"Why, O LORD, do you reject me and hide your face from me?" (Psalm 88:14).

Jeremiah can only understand the destruction of Jerusalem as a result of being abandoned by God. How else could the enemy have defeated them except for the fact that the Lord had "withdrawn his right hand"? (Lamentations 2:3). Only when God looks at, wakes up, remembers, becomes present once more with His people will Israel be restored. His Presence is everything. It is always the ultimate answer.

The deepest experience of this absence of Presence was felt by the One who took upon Himself the sin of the whole world. All that was light, all that was life was gone, had fled, had looked away. At this darkest of all moments, Jesus laments, "Why have You forsaken me?"

In one way or another it is the theme of all lament. It is the confused cry of all who struggle to live in a fallen world where God's perceived absence is the real heart of our battle. It is the opposite of the retreat of denial. Lament is the battle cry!

Rarely do we ask in prayer for what we really need. We usually think a solution will suffice, some sort of answer to our problem. We learn from lament that nothing less than the restored Presence of God will ever satisfy our souls. It is only through lament that we discover how vast the impossible emptiness can feel.

Suggested Bible Readings: Psalm 22; Mark 15:33-39

REFLECT & DISCUSS:

1. Have you ever felt that God was truly absent? How did you respond?

2. What would it be like if you stopped praying for the things you need, and instead prayed only for God's Presence? Could you do it?

HESED

Often, in ancient myth, the traveler is confronted by a closed gate or locked door that can only be opened by means of a mysterious, undefinable word. On our journey of lament this untranslatable word is *hesed*. When the lament is heard, the door opens and God once more fills our awareness with His Presence, the essence of what fills that vast emptiness is called *hesed*.

Hesed is a Hebrew word that describes the indescribable, that defines the undefinable. Put simply, *hesed* is the defining characteristic of God in the Old Testament. Sometimes translated as "loving-kindness," it is a key to understanding who God really is.

Lament happens when we experience suffering that seems inconsistent with God's *hesed*, when the door to His Presence seems locked and barred from the inside. Such moments are often signaled by the word *why*.

Why am I sick?

Why does my enemy triumph over me?

Why did my loved one die?

God, if indeed You are defined by *hesed*, then why . . . ?

At the heart of understanding *hesed* lies the crucial notion that it is unmerited, undeserved, unearnable. This facet of *hesed* is what the New Testament often calls "grace."

Jesus spent so many of His parables trying to define *hesed* for us. The emotional power of the parable of the prodigal son comes from the unexpected forgiveness of the father (see Luke 15:11-32). The twist of the parable of the Good Samaritan is that the person who was not obliged to give anything, gave it all! (see Luke 10:30-37). "Unmerited." "Impossible to earn." God will not wash His hands of us because of His surprising *hesed*. Some other attempts to translate *hesed* include: "enemy-love," "unexpected favor," "surprising grace," "unmerited forgiveness," "unsolicited love," "compassionate grace."

Jesus' life teaches us that a supremely untranslatable word can only be understood when it becomes "infleshed," translated into a living person. Through the incarnation of Jesus, *hesed* was at last perfectly defined. But the call of God for you and me is to continue that incarnating in our own lives. Within the two simple syllables of this indefinable word lay all the richness of the grace and mercy of God. When circumstances cause us to question His *hesed*, we invariably reach out through lament. And somehow, through the mystery of lament, we find it again. Which is to say we find Him again.

🌲🌲🌲

SOME IMPORTANT REFERENCES TO *Hesed*

EXODUS 33:19; ISAIAH 63:9. God shows *hesed* despite Israel's failures.

1 SAMUEL 20:14-17. Jonathan loved David, who should have been his enemy.

DEUTERONOMY 8:11,18. *Hesed* is often tied to remembering. See also Deuteronomy 13:17; 49:10; 2 Samuel 24:14; Psalm 23; 25:6; 40:11; 51:1; 69:16; 79:8; 103:4.

ISAIAH 30:18; 54:8. Explains hiding face motif.

DANIEL 9:9; MICAH 7:19; HABBAKUK 3:2; NEHEMIAH 9:27-28; 13:22. "Remember according to *hesed*."

DEUTERONOMY 30:3; ISAIAH 14:1; 49:10,13; JEREMIAH 12:15; EZEKIEL 39:25. In the *restoration* of the exiles.

DEUTERONOMY 13:17; ISAIAH 54:8; 55:3; JEREMIAH 33:26; MICAH 7:20. His mercy has an eschatological dimension. From God's *hesed* flows the final forgiveness and redemption of His people.

🔻🔻🔻

Suggested Bible Readings: Psalm 136 (the word translated "love" is hesed); Luke 15:11-32

REFLECT & DISCUSS:

1. What situations in your life have caused you to doubt God's *hesed*?

2. How does Jesus perfectly define *hesed*?

FORMULA OF REMEMBRANCE

When a person is lost, it is usually because they have forgotten the way. By the process of remembering they trace their steps back to a more familiar place. In lament, this process is called the formula of remembrance.

In Psalm 42:4, the psalmist interrupts his lament with these words: "These things I remember." In 68:7-18 we read a long remembrance of God's awesome presence among His people. Psalm 74 begins in despair, "Why have you rejected us forever, O God?" but in verse 12 a remembrance begins that speaks of God's power "of old." He "split open the sea" (verse 13) and "crushed the heads of Leviathan" (verse 14). Surely now, the psalmist hopes God will "rise up . . . and defend your cause" (verse 22). Psalm 78, though not a lament, contains a long section looking back on the deeds of God (verses 5-72). Perhaps most interesting is Psalm 136, which contains a long remembrance passage punctuated with communal shouts of *hesed*! (see also Psalms 106; 22:27; 25:5; 40:11; 51:1; 69:16; 79:8; 103:4; 1 Chronicles 16:4). These passages reveal that remembering is also worship.

Remembering can be a powerful path to worship in the midst of disappointment and pain. To look back on those times when God was faithful gives us hope, when in the present sometimes He seems to have hidden His Presence and forgotten His *hesed*.

Lament teaches us that the central question of worship is, "What is God worth?" The formula of remembrance encourages us to ask, "What has God done in my life that's worth remembering?"

In the first chapter of Luke, when Mary first hears she will give birth to the Messiah, she sings a song that includes a "formula of remembrance." Linked to the idea that *Shaddai* has done mighty things in her, Mary recalls other mighty acts of God in the past starting with verse 47. Later Zechariah will use the same formula in his song (see Luke 1:67-79). (It is unfortunate that it is referred to as a "formula," for there are really no formulae in lament. There are, however, forms, and perhaps we would do better to understand remembrance more in these terms.)

Outside of these references, the use of the formula of remembrance in the Old Testament is found almost exclusively in the psalms of lament.

Suggested Bible Readings: Psalm 42; Luke 1:46-56

REFLECT & DISCUSS:

1. What's the benefit of remembering the past, when it's not going to change the future?

2. How does remembrance fit into lament?

VAV ADVERSATIVE

We're almost done with the first week of our journey. You might be tempted to look at the title for today and ask, "What is he thinking?" But wait—it gets better. We're going to talk about Hebrew grammar. "Hebrew grammar!" you're saying to yourself, "What could be helpful about that?" But read on.

Vav is the sixth letter of the Hebrew alphabet. It looks basically like a line with a small flag on the top that always points to the left. ֹ

In the Hebrew language, *vav* connects things. It's usually translated "and." But it has other uses. One of those is called the adversative. Then it is usually translated "but" (or sometimes "yet"), and marks a shift in thinking. (Are you still with me?)

The *vav* adversative occurs frequently in biblical laments. It marks a mysterious transition in the heart and mind of the lamenter. Sometimes you get the feeling that it marks the point at which he simply exhausts himself against God. Sometimes it marks the point at which he stops pouring out complaint and begins to paradoxically pour out praise from his own emptiness. The shift is unpredictable. Sometimes it happens in verse five. Sometimes in verse fifty-five.

When the "crossing of the line" (remember *vav* is a vertical line) occurs, the psalmist dramatically shifts focus from himself and his pain to God and His glory. Often the shift is so abrupt that the only explanation seems to be that God somehow "showed up" and radically transformed the perspective of the one who was lamenting, but who is now worshiping.

***

Here are some of the most striking examples of the *vav* adversative:

Psalm 3, the shift occurs in verse 3
Psalm 13, the shift is in verse 5
Psalm 22, the shift is in verse 19
Psalm 41, the shift is in verse 10
Psalm 55, the shift is in verse 16
Psalm 69, the shift is in verse 13
Psalm 71, the shift is in verse 14
Psalm 73, the shift is in verse 23

Suggested Bible Readings: Psalm 13; Philippians 2:6-11

REFLECT & DISCUSS:

1. How do you think the mysterious "crossing of the line" occurs?

2. Read some of the psalms listed above. What was the author's attitude prior to the shift? What was it after?

JOB: A FRUSTRATED LAMENTER

If you strain to look ahead you'll see him sitting beside the road. At first you might mistake his rounded shoulders and back for a rock. His head is bowed so low it disappears behind his silhouette. As we approach, he turns his head slightly, barely acknowledging our presence.

At this point he has lost everything a man can lose: his children, the respect of his wife and friends, his possessions. Only this morning he noticed a painful lump underneath his skin that an hour ago has begun to ooze. It could be cancer, Ebola, or even AIDS.

Until the moment his world began to fall apart, Job lived his life by a simple equation. He learned it from his mother. It had always "worked." When he was good, he received some sort of reward. The better his performance, the bigger the reward. His parents had always responded to the equation. And up until a few days ago, so had God.

BIBLE BACKGROUND

Job is contained in a collection called the Wisdom Writings (Kethuvim), along with Psalms, Ecclesiastes, Proverbs, and the Song of Solomon. This collection came together during a time of transition in Israel. The shift was not so much political or even religious as it was intellectual and theological. From the beginning, Israel had based her understanding of the world on what some scholars call Torah Obedience. This is the basic understanding that if I keep the Torah, God will bless me—in fact, He is obliged by covenant to do so. If I break any of His laws, He, by necessity, will have to punish me as well as my descendants (see Exodus 34:7). This simple formula gave shape and meaning to Israel's world for centuries.

But then, no one knows just when, questions arose to which this formula had no answers. These questions, which confronted the centuries-old wisdom embodied in Torah Obedience, found a voice in the Writings. And so the collection is not as much about wisdom as the inadequacy of wisdom.

Solomon, for example, bemoans in Ecclesiastes that though he is the wisest man on earth, wisdom is not enough. The Psalms, which we shall see begin with a hymn to Torah Obedience, quickly pass into a series of laments, which give voice to this growing frustration that there are inconsistencies in the fallen world to which Torah Obedience provides no answer.

The best approach to understanding the reason behind this transition is found in what scholars call "progressive revelation." That is, God began to reveal Himself foundationally through the Ten Commandments but progressively continued that process of revelation to His people. It is almost as if, through the tension created by the Wisdom Writings, God is saying, "How could you believe that a giver of commandments was all I am?" And so, if this idea is correct, God revealed more and more of Himself as time went on. He showed Himself to be a Father and even a Mother to His people. He went on to reveal Himself as a Friend to some, like Moses and Abraham. Eventually, through the Incarnation, He would reveal Himself most completely and intimately as the Bridegroom who loves us so much He wants to be married to us!

Job represents a major step in this process. The tensions that exist between Job and his wife and friends illustrate how painful the process of revelation can be for God's people. As a reward for his suffering, Job will catch a few glimpses of Jesus. They represent some of the most striking images of Jesus in the Old Testament (see Job 9:33; 16:19; 19:25).

Usually people read Job asking the question, "Who is right?" "Is it Elihu?" "Is it Job?" The fact is, none of them are completely right about God. Because the book of Job is not about being right, it is about being faithful.

For the purpose of our study, try instead to understand Job as a frustrated lamenter, as someone who seeks, again and again, to reach out to God through lament but who is interrupted time and time again by his friends. They repeatedly drag Job into theological discussions about God. But Job needs to talk to God. By the end of their long dialogue you'll see that Job has almost let go and given up on God. "I'll never find Him," he says. Just then, in the nick of time, God appears!

Through the process of the divine questioning, God reveals that He cannot be contained in a simple definition or equation. At the same time He unveils His awesomeness but also that He is a God who is moved by Job's tears and ours. It is a tremendous step forward in the revelation of His true character and it would have never happened if Job had not stubbornly reached out to God through the process of lament.

THE STORY

READ: JOB 1:1–2:10

Make sure you dwell on the very first verse. It tells us all we need to know about the unfortunate man from the land of Uz whom we will be following for the next two weeks. He is blameless. The narrator says so. God will say so as well in verse 8. And he fears God, which the Wisdom Writings tells us is the beginning of wisdom (see Proverbs 9:10). Because of his uprightness and fear of God, Job shuns evil. This is where the journey, Job's and ours, begins. If fear is the beginning of wisdom, where might the end lie?

The throne room scene, which begins in verse 6, gives us, the readers, precious information that poor Job has to struggle without knowing Satan, the Accuser, accuses Job of only fearing God because God has blessed him for it. Take the blessing away and Job will let go of God. And so the story begins to unfold.

REFLECT & DISCUSS:

1. What is your initial reaction when you read Job 1:12 or 2:6? Why do you think God would allow Satan to test Job's relationship with God?

2. Look at Job 1:13-18. Now put yourself in Job's place. How would your response to a similar trial compare to Job's response (in 1:21-22)?

3. Job 2:4-8 probably hits close to home if you've suffered from physical ailments (or are close to someone who is suffering). Is Satan speaking the truth when he claims that faith is tested most when a person suffers physical harm? Explain.

THREE FRIENDS

READ: JOB 2:11-13

Job's three friends, Eliphaz, Bildad, and Zophar, arrive in chapter 2. They have come to sympathize with their dear, suffering brother. They are prepared to sit in silence in the presence of his great suffering. They reveal the truth of how difficult it is to find meaningful words in the face of genuine suffering. One wonders how long they would have endured along with Job. It is finally Job who breaks the silence. From this point on they will respond to his laments.

REFLECT & DISCUSS:

1. What practical lessons can you learn from the example of Job's friends? When you encounter someone who is suffering now, what will you do differently?

2. Isn't it appropriate to respond in words to the suffering of our friends and family?

FIRST LAMENT

READ: JOB 3

Job's first lament is an extended curse on the day he was born. He begins at the beginning and realizes that it would have truly been better if he had never been born. These are not exactly suicidal thoughts, but they come as close as possible.

"What I feared has come upon me (verse 25)," he sighs at the end of the lament. His life, which had been lived in the fear of God, now seems to be fragmenting. He has lost much: his possessions and especially his children, all that seemed to give meaning to his life. But what he laments most it seems, is the loss of the hope he had for life itself.

REFLECT & DISCUSS:

1. This lament is Job's response to his second test (physical affliction). How does it differ from his response to his first test? (See Job 1:20-22.) Why the change in attitude?

2. Have you ever, like Job, truly wished you were dead or had never been born? What was your response to that feeling?

SECOND AND THIRD LAMENT

READ: JOB 6:1–7:21; 10:1-22

After Eliphaz's chastising response to his first lament, Job lashes back, not so much at Eliphaz as toward God. "Let Him crush me," he goads. His friend has posited the notion that Job must be suffering for something he has done. "Who, being innocent, has ever perished?" he reasons (4:7). The inescapable conclusion: Job must not be innocent.

But note how Job refuses to let go of his lament, which is to say he refuses to let go of God. He refuses to restrain his words to God, though his friends will warn him again and again not to speak in such ways to God. Job is a picture of a man caught between the rationalizations and theologizing of his friends and his own attempt to wrestle with God through lament. Eventually he will be so distracted by the arguments of his friends that he will cease reaching out to God at all (compare 23:3).

By the end of his second lament Job turns frontally toward God. It is a significant shift. "Why have *you* made me your target?" he pleads (7:20).

(Following his second lament, Bildad responds to his friend Job in chapter 8. His position is basically the same as Eliphaz: that is, Job must be guilty to be suffering so. In chapter 9 Job ceases to lament and begins to reason with his friend. It is significant that God is no longer "You" but "He.")

In chapter 10 Job begins his third lament. It opens with another stubborn statement that he will "speak out in the bitterness of [his] soul." Job refuses to rein in either his emotions or his language. This lament is full of "ifs" and "whys."

REFLECT & DISCUSS:

1. If you have ever been chastised by a friend for your lament, how did you respond? What do you think prompted your friend's reprimand?

2. How comfortable were you with Job's brutally honest pleading with God? Have you ever launched a frontal "attack" on God like Job's? If so, what prompted that? How was the situation resolved, if at all?

Speaking the Language of Lament for Yourself

Now that you have had a week to be introduced to the world of lament, spend today looking back on the passages you have read. What images have remained in your mind over time? Where do you sense clarity and where is there still confusion?

Journaling provides a wonderful means of prayer. Allow the themes and language that have worked their way into your own prayer life to be put down on paper. Perhaps you are beginning to experience a new sense of freedom before God. You have learned from lament that you can and should offer Him everything as an act of worship.

Locate those sorrows in your life that are central. Family, health, money. Where have you experienced suffering? What have you feared most?

Job's experience seems unique in Scripture. Is it? You probably know someone (perhaps that someone is you) who has experienced all kinds of tragedy and pain. Someone who has experienced Job-like trials. Is Job's experience a test or does God know he will remain faithful? And what about those people you know with similar experiences? What is God's role in the suffering?

Spend some time in prayer, asking for God's grace and guidance as you begin to practice lament. Then write your lament in the following space. Spill out all of the stuff that came to the surface as you've studied. Don't hold back from God in this.

JOB: THE COMPLETION OF THE EQUATION

Perhaps by now the implication of the original equation of Job and his friends is becoming clear to you. If a person is good, that person will be blessed by God. If the person is not good that person will receive His curse. God is reduced by this equation to One who merely responds to the actions of His creatures. He is rendered predictable. This has the greatest appeal for those who embrace the original equation.

When suffering entered Job's life, the safe element of predictability vanished with it. The thought is frightening to Job's friends, as they stand by and look on, trying to figure it all out. If Job is suffering for something he does not deserve, then a vital piece of the equation must be missing. Finding that piece is what the remainder of the book of Job is about.

FOURTH LAMENT

READ: JOB 13:17–14:22

We left Job lamenting his innocence in chapter 10. Zophar will respond in chapter 11, "God has overlooked *some* of your iniquity" (verse 6), but "the eyes of the wicked pine away" (verse 20). The implication: Job is clearly "pine-ing," therefore he must be wicked.

In chapter 12, Job responds to Zophar's insinuations. Once again it is vital to see that he has ceased talking to God and is merely talking *about* Him once more. The Lord has become the subject of an extended conversation, no longer the object of Job's lament.

Around 13:17 (it seems difficult to pinpoint just where), Job makes the vital turn back toward the God with whom he is so frustrated. He asks for two concessions: first that God will take away His hand and so stop frightening Job with all His "terrors." Second, that a face-to-face discussion might begin between the two of them. This fourth lament appears to be largely a matter of Presence.

REFLECT & DISCUSS:

1. What do you think caused Job to turn back around toward God in his lament?

2. Think back on a recent time in your life when you might have lamented. What concessions would you have asked for? Why these?

FIFTH LAMENT

READ: JOB 29:1–31:40

In chapter 15, Eliphaz speaks for a second time but his message has not changed. Job should not speak to God in such language (15:12-13) and bad people suffer (15:20).

As Job struggles to respond to Eliphaz in 16–17, twice he breaks free and briefly speaks directly to God, in 16:7-8 and 17:3-4. In the first attempt, he confesses that God has "worn him out." In the second, he begs for God to give him the "pledge" God Himself has demanded. Job has begun to sense that what he is supposed to give *to* God, he will only receive *from* God.

Bildad and Zophar will both speak again as well, and Job will respond to their theologizing as best he knows how.

The language of lament reappears in 29:1. It is significant that Job's final lament begins directly after a restatement of the basic tenant with which the book began, "The fear of the Lord—that is wisdom" (28:28).

This lament wanders through several verses before it finally finds the strength to turn once more back to God in 30:20. What follows is another extended series of "ifs." With these frustrated attempts at self-justification the words of Job come to an end.

REFLECT & DISCUSS:

1. Which is the greater challenge for Job in this section: responding to Eliphaz or wrestling with God? What does this tell you about the role friends play in the process of lament?

2. Think about the self-justification you have attempted in the middle of lament. What caused you to do that? What value was there in expressing these thoughts?

THE DIVINE QUESTIONS

READ: JOB 38:1–40:2; 42:7-9

Elihu appears out of the blue in chapter 32. The last time we tasted narrative was chapter 3! (Everything else has been dialogue.) Now we are introduced to the young, intelligent Elihu, from whom we hope for so much. For six long chapters he speaks without taking a breath. His language is often beautiful. He recounts many of Job's major points, which shows us he was listening after all. But in the end he simply restates the original equation of retributive justice (34:11; 36:11-12) and chides Job for speaking to God through lament (34:36).

We have been listening to these five men talk about God for thirty-five chapters now. (God has not spoken since chapter 2!) What seems clear is that we have arrived at the end of human wisdom. His friends are out of words to say. Job is out of tears. Has a stage ever been better set for God to appear and speak?

Though Job has been crying out for answers, answers are not what God knows he needs. And so God appears with a legion of impossible questions for Job. They are, all of them, unanswerable.

REFLECT & DISCUSS:

1. When God finally reappears at the end of the book, His only response to Job's questions are more questions. What do you think this response tells us about the nature of God?

2. Do you think that today you and I might have this same experience in prayer, of having our questions answered with more questions? Could questions paradoxically represent the best answers or are they supposed to function in such a way as to drive us back to God?

3. In the end of the book, Job gets his stuff back. Does this really support the idea that God always blesses the good and always curses the bad? If the conclusion does not support this idea, then what do you think it is there for?

THE COSTLY VISION

READ: JOB 9:33-35; 16:19-21; 19:25-27

Three enormous statements of faith with waves of lament breaking around their feet rise out of the sea of Job's suffering. Three times he is granted a vision of the coming Jesus, which will not be equaled in clarity until the time of Isaiah.

Yet none of these statements occur within the passages we have labeled lament. Instead, all of them seem to erupt from Job's fiery responses to his friends, who have become his accusers.

JOB 9:33-35

If only there were someone to arbitrate between us,
　　to lay his hand upon us both,
　　someone to remove God's rod from me,
　　　so that his terror would frighten me no more.
Then I would speak up without fear of him.

If the equation is incomplete, then this must represent the missing piece. If I cannot be good enough, then I need someone to stand between myself and God. Notice how, in the presence of this Arbitrator, the initial state of fear, where wisdom began, seems to disappear.

JOB 16:19-21

Even now my witness is in heaven;
my Advocate is on high.
　　My Intercessor is my friend
as my eyes pour out tears to God;
　　on behalf of a man he pleads with God
as a man pleads for his friend.

The Arbitrator is now revealed as Advocate. As He intercedes for Job, Job realizes the unthinkable: this Person is also his Friend! What other response is appropriate but tears? As Job weeps before the God whom he no longer fears, he discovers that his Friend is pleading for him.

JOB 19:25-27

I know that my Redeemer lives,
>   and that in the end he will stand upon the earth.
> And after my skin has been destroyed,
>   yet in my flesh I will see God;
>   I myself will see him with my own eyes—I, and not another.
> How my heart yearns within me!

The final realization is that this Friend/Advocate/Arbitrator really exists! He is alive, not some figment of Job's tormented imagination. Above his present despair, all of his losses and pain, Job is given the vision of a time when he will stand together with his Redeemer on the earth. God, who before the vision was death to see, will be clearly beheld by Job's new eyes. It is what his heart has really been yearning for all along, not answers, not vindication—but Presence.

REFLECT & DISCUSS:

1. What do you make of Job's Christological statements? How did his suffering play a part in allowing him to make these realizations? Could he have made them without his pain?

2. What is the fundamental characteristic of the "Redeemer" he saw?

SPEAKING THE LANGUAGE OF LAMENT FOR YOURSELF

In the final chapter of the book of Job (42:7-17), God charges the three friends, "you have not spoken of me what is right as my servant Job has (verse 7)." They are ordered to make a sacrifice and ask Job to pray to God for them (verse 8). "After Job had prayed for his friends," God restored Job's fortunes twofold. In a sense, Job becomes for his theologizing friends like the intercessor and advocate he had seen in his vision.

Job's other friends come to a meal to honor him, giving him gifts of gold. His sheep and cattle are restored. He has seven more sons and three beautiful daughters. He lives 140 years, living to see four generations of his family. He dies "old and content."

After all Job lost, after all he endured, in the end of the book his possessions are restored twofold. He gains once more the admiration of his friends. And though he will never get back the children he originally lost, God grants him more sons and daughters. But more importantly, in the end of the story, Job gets God back!

In regard to your own experience of suffering, what has Job taught you? From this point on how will you respond when sorrow or confusion enters your life? Will you feel the freedom to voice your complaints to God? Has Job, in some way, taught you a new language for honestly pouring out your heart to God?

As you compose your lament, reflect on the question: Do you only suffer for doing something bad? Sometimes? Never?

DAVID: A LIFE FASHIONED FOR LAMENT

We part company with Job and his feasting friends, moving thoughtfully further down the path we first set our feet on three weeks ago. Our friend from the land of Uz made us aware of a depth of anguish many of us didn't know could exist. He represented innocent suffering and began to teach us the only language that can respond honestly to God without letting go.

On the next rise, someone stands waiting to join us for the next leg of the journey. Though he is a man, he has the face of a boy. He holds a lyre in one hand and a stylus in the other and seems eager to meet up with us. He is both a shepherd and a king, the composer and the singer of more laments than anyone.

If ever a life was fashioned for lament, it was David's life. Born in the deserted wilderness of Bethlehem, he was the youngest of eight brothers. The stories of his childhood confirm what we have come to know of last-born children. He was ignored. He was looked down upon. When Samuel came to anoint one of Jesse's sons as king, no one even considered David. The effects of this lonely childhood shape many of David's laments. When he sings, as he so often does, about forsakenness, there is a resonance in his laments that would have never been there otherwise.

His laments often turn toward the subject of his enemies. Once again, David's troubled life had given him more than enough experience with enemies. Hadn't his own brothers treated him like enemies? Even as a boy, David found himself cast into the midst of a grown-up battle with the Philistines, surrounded by enemies, one of whom was, of course, the giant Goliath.

His first job was for a man who would become his bitterest enemy, Saul. David's skill at playing the harp and composing music led him to a position as court musician. His music was the only medicine that would soothe Saul's sick mind. In time, the king would hate David for all the strengths for which everyone else seemed to love him.

David lived long enough to see the death of everyone he had ever loved. We hear him lamenting the deaths of two of his sons. Most poignantly, he laments the deaths of Jonathan, the man he loved the most, and Jonathan's father, Saul, the man who hated him the most. The song of lament, in 2 Samuel 1, pays tribute to the heart of David, who mourns for his worst enemy with as much sorrow as his dearest friend.

Through it all, David lamented sin that was done to him. But these are not the most important laments he has to teach us. On the most significant part of this journey, he will lead us into the dark territory of our own sin. There David will help teach us the only language that will keep us connected to the Redeemer Job saw. David will teach us the lament of repentance.

Loneliness, sorrow, disease, and death, and most especially personal sin: They would all become themes of lament from a life so supremely gifted and at the same time so tremendously troubled.

BIBLE BACKGROUND

Second Samuel 6 and 1 Chronicles 13–16 describe David's role in bringing the ark back to Jerusalem and his leadership in reestablishing the worship of the Lord. The chronicler tells us he was responsible for the appointment of "singers to sing joyful songs, accompanied by musical instruments: lyres, harps and cymbals" (1 Chronicles 15:16). Soon after that, the details are made even more specific: "They were to play the lyres and the harps, Asaph was to sound the cymbals, and Benaiah and Jahaziel the priests were to blow the trumpets regularly before the ark of the covenant of God" (16:5-6). All this, apparently at David's direction.

In 1 Chronicles 16:7 we read a tantalizing hint, "That day David first committed to Asaph and his associates this psalm of thanks to the LORD." What follows is a magnificent inaugural hymn that opened a new era in the worship of Israel. We have seen that David's first real "job" was that of a musician (see 1 Samuel 16:18). Today we are only coming to realize the power of the "music therapy" that David seemed to understand all those centuries ago.

When we read the superscriptions that appear before roughly 117 of the 150 psalms and note that the majority of these include the phrase "of David," the fact becomes clear that he was the key figure not only in reorganizing worship but also composing the songs that were used in the new "ark-shrine" he built in his new capital, Jerusalem.

A FUTURE KING

READ: 1 SAMUEL 16

As we have seen, the context of lament begins for us early in life. Our own experiences of aloneness (hunger for Presence) and the deep sense that the world is not the way it should be go as far back as our memories can reach.

As chapter 16 opens, we see that Samuel has been lamenting the lost kingship of Saul. In 15:34 we had been told of the prophet's final departure from the king. Even the Lord, we are told, is grieving over the king, lamenting that He had ever made him king in the first place. (See 1 Samuel 8:7-8, where God laments the people's rejection of Him as king.)

Early in chapter 16, when first we meet the young David, he is the youngest son in a large family of sons. He is the smallest and by everyone's reckoning, the least promising of all of Jesse's sons. We see the prophet Samuel sent by God to find the young, new king, *in the wilderness*.

Seven of Jesse's sons pass before Samuel, all of them promising young men, already warriors in their own right. But the Lord rejects them all. Finally, as an afterthought, David is sent for. His handsome face is flushed from running all the way. It seems he is not used to being called for.

"He is the one," says the Lord. And so it begins. The Spirit of the Lord comes on the young boy in power. It will remain with David for the rest of his life. (See the amazing oath God makes to David in Psalm 89.)

David, the incognito king, enters the service of Saul, who is tormented by an evil spirit. David's first job is as therapeutic musician to Saul. It was a fitting school for the one who would compose so many songs of comfort and lament.

REFLECT & DISCUSS:

1. What is your reaction to God's lament that He had even made Saul king in the first place? What does this tell you about God? About lament?

2. Think about the origins of lament in David's life. What parallels can you draw to your own childhood?

A LAMENT FOR AN ENEMY AND A FRIEND

READ: 2 SAMUEL 1

One of the bitterest ironies of David's life is that his best friend, Jonathan, was the son of his worst enemy, Saul. In so many of his laments we will see David trying to cope with his fear and hatred for his many enemies.

In this first chapter of 2 Samuel, we read of a nameless Amalekite, probably someone scavenging on the battlefield at Mount Gilboa. He comes to tell David that he, in obedience to Saul's command, has killed the king and brought his crown and armband to David. David and all his men tore their clothes and "mourned and wept and fasted" (verse 12). Apparently, during this time he composes a lament, perhaps using his bow string as a crude instrument. He commands that all the men of Judah memorize it.

What I hope you will find most stunning is the complete absence of any kind of bitterness when he laments his enemy Saul. David describes him with as much affection as he does his dear friend, Jonathan. In this early lament, we see that David has refused to allow Saul's hatred to impact him. Though the first king had sought to kill David again and again, David seems to harbor no hatred for Saul in his heart. How was David able to come to such a place of freedom in his emotional life? It would almost seem as if he had come to love his enemy, as Jesus would later command His disciples to do. How David was able to arrive at this place is one of the most important questions we must answer as we look at lament.

REFLECT & DISCUSS:

1. What difference is there, if any, between the lament expressed for an enemy and the one expressed for a friend? Why is this significant?

2. Why do you think David was able to lament without bitterness on the death of Saul? Do you think you could do this? Why or why not?

A LAMENT BEYOND WORDS

READ: 2 SAMUEL 18

This passage contains another important lament for an enemy, only this time the enemy was David's own son, Absalom. In 2 Samuel 15 we read the story of the birth of the conspiracy of David's son. He secretly enlists Ahithophel, the grandfather of the ill-treated Bathsheba, to help in the betrayal. (Some scholars believe David's laments in Psalms 41 and 55 contain traces of this story.)

David flees Jerusalem, amidst the mourning people of the countryside. During the flight from the city, it is clear that David understands that this trouble has come upon him as a result of his own sin. Perhaps his trusted adviser, Ahithophel's, participation in the plot reminded him once more of his sin against Bathsheba, Uriah, and especially the Lord. David clearly understands that this might very well be a part of the punishment he deserves. (See also the cursing of Shimei in 16:5-14.)

Later Absalom dies a bizarre death at the hand of Joab, David's commander. The first messenger brings the good news that those who were fighting against the king have been defeated. "But what about Absalom?" David asks. "I don't know," he responds. Finally a second messenger arrives with news that Absalom is dead.

Of all his heartbroken laments, this seems the most intense. Certainly he mourns the death of his son, but given the events that led up to the rebellion, one wonders if the depth of David's grief was the hand he himself had taken in the whole bloody business. Could Absalom be just another in a long dark line that began with Uriah?

Listen closely to the lament in 2 Samuel 18:33 and its echo in 19:4. Note the brevity, the lack of poetry. This is not a lament that would ever be set to music. It is beyond David's remarkable gift of words. It is absolutely vital that we experience this moment with the greatest composer of lament. The deepest of our griefs, those beyond words, must still be offered to God.

REFLECT & DISCUSS:

1. Have you ever felt like David—that the reason for your lament is (at least in part) punishment for your sins? How do you resolve that feeling?

2. Consider the lack of poetry in some of David's laments. What does this say about your own lamenting? What comfort is there in knowing that your beyond-words laments are welcomed by God?

A BRIEF INTRODUCTION TO DAVID'S LAMENT PSALMS

The Psalms represent a collection of collections. The overall structure falls into five books. Most scholars believe this outline is meant to mirror the structure of the Five Books of Moses or the Torah. Within these five books several authors are represented, among them Solomon (Psalms 72; 127) and Moses (Psalm 90). By far, however, David authored most of the book, 117 of the 150 psalms. (Several of the psalms that bear no composer's name in their title are no doubt David's as well.)

Scholars like Erhard Gerstenberger, Claus Westermann, and most recently Walter Brueggemann, have pointed out a progression in the structure of the Psalms. The collection opens with a preface in Psalm 1 that is dedicated to the Torah. The final six psalms of the collection form a conclusion of almost riotous praise. Approximately in the middle, at the opening of book three, lies Psalm 73. In this psalm, approximately halfway through the collection, Brueggemann has found a representative lament that marks the middle of the transition from Psalm 1 to Psalm 150. He pointedly asks the question, "How do you get from a psalm of Torah obedience to a psalm of unbroken praise?" He finds a part of the answer in Psalm 73, which beautifully represents what a lament is all about. (See Brueggemann's *The Psalms: The Life of Faith*.)

It opens with a statement of the old notion that if one is pure in heart then God will respond by being good to them in return. What follows is the same struggle we saw in Job and will see in Habakkuk, Ecclesiastes, and other parts of the Wisdom Books. That is, the psalmist is troubled that the old equation seems not to function in the real world; the arrogant and wicked seem to prosper (verses 3-12). He is tempted to believe that he has kept his heart pure for nothing (verses 13-16). The lament turns around in verse 17 (though not by means of a *vav* adversative). "Til I entered the sanctuary of God," Asaph says. From this point on the clouds begin to part, clarity comes once more to the point that from verse 23 to the end of the psalm we hear some of the most intimate words of praise in the psalter. If the collection of the psalms represents a deliberate journey from 1 to 150, then 73 represents a major signpost along the pathway.

Most of the other mile markers along the way are laments of David. Each one, in its own unique way, represents another small step in this journey of progressive revelation, in this voyage that begins in the wilderness with a

God of obedience and finds its fulfillment in a throne room before the Lord
whom we praise for His *hesed*.

READ: PSALM 55

FROM TERROR TO TRUST

Of all the difficult burdens those in leadership must bear, the most difficult
may be the betrayal of those who were thought to be friends. David faced
this sort of treachery again and again, even from members of his own family.
Many scholars believe that this psalm of lament was written during the
struggle against Absalom.

It is vital to see the progression that is represented in the psalm: the
movement from fear and trembling, to testimony, to trust. In the process,
David has voiced his complaint concerning his enemy and has ultimately
handed him over to God. Penultimately, he testifies to the truth that God
can indeed be trusted in this most desperate of circumstances.

This lament illustrates what can be said to be true about the entire
psalter; it is taking us *somewhere*. From fear to confidence, from obedience
(Psalm 1) to praise (Psalm 150).

REFLECT & DISCUSS:

1. As we meditate on this, our first psalm, it would be good to ask God
   just where He desires to take us. Where are you right now? In a place
   of fear? In the wilderness? In a place where you thought all God ever
   wanted from you was obedience?

2. And where might He be taking you? Through a dark valley to someplace beyond? To a place where you might discover a real relationship
   with Him? Could such a thing even be possible?

SPEAKING THE LANUGAGE OF
LAMENT FOR YOURSELF

As we reach this, halfway point, now is a good time to reassess just where we've been. What has the journey been like for you thus far? Where have you come from? Where do you sense God leading you? At this point along the way are there themes of lament in your own life that have surfaced? What do you regret? What sin in your own life has come to light along the way? Have you offered up your lament as an act of worship?

As thoughts for lament do begin to surface remember those qualities we saw in Job and David. They existed in marvelous freedom before God. They possessed a stubborn refusal to turn away from God. They understood with their hearts as well as their minds that God's character was defined by *hesed*. They realized that, most of all, they needed Presence. Do you? Do I? As you write your own laments, describe what that yearning for Presence feels like in your own life.

DAVID: COMPOSER OF LAMENT

David's psalms cover the entire spectrum of lament. He wonders why God is absent (in his perception), and asks "how long" God will hide His face. He questions why a God of *hesed* allows so much tragedy in the world. In some psalms, he laments and then moves to praise. In others, he starts off confident, but for some reason begins to doubt. He laments his own sin.

David discovered that unlamented sin — that is, denial — can destroy your spiritual life. Hidden sin simply gives the Devil more power over us. But when sin is confessed and its darkness lamented before God, it becomes repentance. And Satan is robbed of that particular hold on us.

"HOW LONG?"

READ: PSALM 13

If it is true that the heart of most lament has to do with a perceived absence of God's Presence, then the question that most often comes to the surface is "How long?" How long will God hide His face? How long will He look away? When will He "show up"? (The other major question "Why?" comes inevitably as a result of a perceived inconsistency in regard to God's *hesed*.)

Until God's Presence is once more experienced, David's enemies will continue to triumph over him. He will continue to wrestle with his tormenting thoughts. The same could be said of you and me. When our circumstances or our feelings point to the possibility that God is not present, nothing seems to go right, for indeed without Him nothing ever could. We focus on the pain, the difficulties, or the guilt over our sin, focusing entirely on the circumstances. What must eventually happen is for us to wake up, turn around, and cross the line from self-focus to God-focus. This is precisely the line that David crosses in verse five of Psalm 13. It is, of course, the line of the *vav* adversative.

"But I trust in your [*hesed*]" (verse 5). As he affirms in faith what he believes to be true about God, notice how the situation completely changes. The circumstances might or might not have changed, but the condition of David's heart is utterly different. The object of his focus has changed. The lament has taken him somewhere; from frustration to praise.

The *vav* adversative does not represent a literary, technical formula. It provides an indication that God had done something: granted faith to the psalmist, where before there was none. While every lament in Scripture is God's Word, it does not always, strictly speaking, represent His voice. God allows the psalmist to voice his dark feelings in order to provide a situation where faith becomes possible.

From this point in the psalm, all we hear is praise.

REFLECT & DISCUSS:

1. David asks of God, "How long will you hide your face from me?" (verse 1). Does God really hide His face? Or is it a human problem of perception?

2. What is the theme of the praise with which David ends this psalm? What has he discovered that is praiseworthy?

A LAMENT OF REPENTANCE

READ: PSALM 51; 2 SAMUEL 11–12

Lament is born from our desperation in light of a perceived absence of God, ✳
out of our desire to reconnect with Him. Sin is the primary barrier that
separates us from God. As we have seen, our only hope lies in His *hesed*, in
His grace. Psalm 51 seems to be the point where these realizations all came
together for David.

Of all the psalms that contain an historical superscription, this is the one
we know best. The experience that brought forth this psalm of contrition
was David's sin with Bathsheba (see 2 Samuel 11).

The issue of transgression is between David and God alone. All sin is
ultimately sin against God, even as the remedy for sin is only with God. In
the depth of his lament, David receives this disturbing clarity from beyond
himself. He multiplies his requests for God's work in his sinful life: "Purge
me," "wash me," "hide your face from my sins," "blot out," "create," "renew,"
"do not cast away," "restore," "sustain," "deliver," "open my lips."

Psalm 51:16 contains the shadows of a new understanding, a progressive
revelation. The conventional sacrifice of a burnt offering, David is beginning
to understand, is not ultimately what God wants. The prescribed sacrifices
are only a pattern, a symbol for what God has really wanted all along. It is the
most costly lesson David ever learned. After experiencing the devastating
effects of his sin, all David has left is a broken spirit and a broken heart. All
he has left is all God really wanted all along!

REFLECT & DISCUSS:

1. On what does David base his appeal to God in Psalm 51:1? What
   allows David to hope for mercy?

2. Why does David say that he has only sinned against God? Don't we sin
   against other people, too?

FROM CONFIDENCE TO DOUBT

READ: PSALM 27

There are no formulae in lament, even as in our emotional lives there are no set patterns. Most often we move from doubt and fear, through faith, toward confidence in the Lord. This is the progression we see most often in biblical lament. But sometimes we move in the other direction. Initially we stand strong but as the shadows of our enemies appear over the horizon, we are tempted to doubt. This reversal is shadowed in Psalm 27.

David begins with a confident proclamation in the light and salvation of the Lord. He has tasted them in his life, so why should he ever have reason to fear? The language of battle speaks of David's many victories as a warrior king (verses 2-3). The language of intimacy with the Lord speaks of the closeness of his past relationship (verses 4-5). David promises to offer sacrifices, to sing and make melody. His service follows closely after his experience of closeness with the Lord.

In verse 7 a mysterious and subtle turn occurs. He utters a cry that he might be heard. In the next verse, something in David's heart compels him to look desperately for God's face. The plea intensifies as the face of God seems to become hidden. In fear David pleads that God will not hide, turn away, cast him off, or forsake him. Perhaps the reason for the shift from confidence to doubt is that David's enemies have reappeared.

Toward the end of the psalm, David seems to be repeating to himself, as much as to us, words of determined hope: "I believe," "I will see," "wait," "be strong," "take courage." Though the psalm shifted to doubt, it does not end without hope.

REFLECT & DISCUSS:

1. What could account for the subtle loss of confidence illustrated in this psalm? Can you think of a situation in your own life in which you started off with great faith, and then began doubting? How did you handle it?

2. What does this lament teach us about doubt and confidence? What does the apparently backward movement in emotion tell us? (Hint: How does the psalm end?)

"WHY?"

READ: PSALM 22

Psalm 22 represents one of the darkest laments in the psalter. The superscription to this psalm says it is to be performed to a lost tune entitled "The Doe of the Morning." It is difficult to imagine singing such a dark, agonizing lyric to a tune with such a gentle title.

It contains every important element we have seen in the psalms of lament. The core issue of the lament is the lack of Presence and the deep anguish that comes as a result of trying to understand "why" a God of *hesed* would allow such a thing. This psalm provides for us a new definition for the word *hell*. It is the hidden face of God.

In addition to the torment of the perceived absence of God, David sings of the despairing silence of God. The Formula of Remembrance gives some hope as David recalls that in the past God listened (verses 3-5). His tortures include scorn, being despised and mocked. It seems as if David, in the throes of his suffering, lashes back and forth between his torments and the frail hope to which he still clings. He returns to the idea that even from birth, God had been there, keeping him safe. David provides in Psalm 22 the most detailed description of the Crucifixion that can be found in all the Bible, more detailed even than the ones in the Gospels.

In verse 19 the long awaited shift occurs (the *vav* adversative). As always, the shift is from a focus on suffering to the hope of God. "But you, O LORD . . . " And with the crossing of this line, the darkness appears to begin mercifully lifting.

In verse 24, the reasons for the shift are given. In the end, God did not hide, and He did hear. The experience of forsakenness in the opening verse has vanished in light of the fact that God's face is seen once more.

The lament concludes with a long passage of praise. The psalmist reaches out to every conceivable group with his praise: the congregation, the poor, those who seek him, the ends of the earth, all the families of the nations, even all who sleep in death! And finally, those as yet unborn, all of them will praise the Lord. The movement of Psalm 22 is from the darkest dark to the brightest light. From the blackest, most forsaken suffering of Jesus Christ as He took upon Himself the sin of the world, to the eventual experience He had of the "joy set before him" (Hebrews 12:2).

On an infinitely smaller scale, this psalm charts the path we too must walk: from the painful experience of the effect of our own sin to the glorious freedom that only comes from breaking through the darkness of that impenetrable cloud and into the glory of Presence. This psalm definitely intends to take us someplace: from the foot of the cross of Jesus to a place before the Throne of the Presence!

REFLECT & DISCUSS:

1. How do you understand David's intimate experience of Jesus' sufferings as they are reflected in Psalms 22 and 69?

2. Where do questions like "why?" and "how long?" ultimately come from? Fallenness? Selfishness? What does lament teach us to do with such questions?

SPEAKING THE LANGUAGE OF LAMENT FOR YOURSELF

Now is a good time to look back to see where you've been in this journey of lament, to see how far you've come and where you think you're headed. Has the language of lament made its way into your personal prayer time? Has it impacted your relationship with God?

At this point perhaps you are ready to ask yourself the question suggested to us by the Formula of Remembrance: "What has God done in my life that is worth remembering?" Hopefully, this question will move you in the direction of seeing the "worth-ship" of God in your own life. Ponder this as you compose your lament.

JEREMIAH: A DIFFICULT HOPE

The pathway of lament that we've been following these five weeks leads us now to the gates of ancient Jerusalem. All seems to be "business as usual." Merchants are coming and going with their wares. The priests are busy about their duties in the Temple Courts. The people pass us by seemingly without a care in the world.

And then we spot him, standing beside the same road we're on. All the cares that were so visibly absent on their faces are disturbingly clear on his. The sense of holiness we thought we missed in the Temple is gathered around him like the dark cloud of the Presence on the mountain of Moses. His eyes are full of tears as he cries out to the people passing by. They seem to be deaf to his pleading. Could it be that they have become used to not listening to Jeremiah, "the weeping prophet"?

He notices something familiar in our faces, in yours and mine. It is almost as if he is afraid to believe that we might believe, that we might listen to him; that we might want to join him on his painful path of lament.

At the end of his long and difficult life we will find Jeremiah standing amidst the rubble of Jerusalem, amidst the wreckage of his own life as well, for he is the only prophet of whom it might be said that the destruction he predicted destroyed him as well. And yet, he survived. How he was able to do this is one of the most important questions we can ask of his lamentable life.

BIBLE BACKGROUND

The book that bears his name is the longest in all of the Bible (it has the most words). We know more about him than any other Old Testament prophet, indeed more than almost any single character of the Old Testament, except perhaps David. He was born in the poverty stricken village of Anathoth, in the territory of Benjamin, a forever impoverished part of the country — all desert and deserted, the way his life would turn out.

Sadly, the Lord commanded him not to marry (see Jeremiah 16:1-4), due, no doubt, to the perilous times in which he lived. His only real friend seems to have been his scribe, Baruch, who wrote the concluding chapter of his prophecy.

His was a most lamentable life. All but one of the kings to which he was sent to speak the Word of the Lord refused to listen. One of them,

Jehoiakim, literally burned his writings (see Jeremiah 36:23). But this did not defeat Jeremiah, who, at the Lord's command, simply rewrote the book, even adding to it.

In fact, nothing seems to have been able to defeat Jeremiah. (His name is thought to mean "the Lord casts down.") The ill will of the people, even the experience of being abandoned by God Himself, was not able to cast down this remarkable man.

We might be tempted to think of Jeremiah in this light as a rugged individual. Nothing could be farther from the truth. He is known as the "weeping prophet." Again and again in his prophecies and in his book, Lamentations, we hear his tender heart break.

A COSTLY CALL

READ: JEREMIAH I

The call to be a prophet is a costly call. To speak the words of God to a people who historically had seldom cared to listen was not a role Jeremiah savored. The call came when he was still a young man. The Lord's first words to him affirmed that He had known Jeremiah before he was formed in the womb. Before he was born, he had been set apart as a "prophet to the nations" (verse 5). Jeremiah tried to escape the call of God on his life by pointing to his youth. Like Moses, he also claimed that he did not know how to speak, so how could he possibly be qualified to speak for God? The Lord would not listen to either of these excuses.

"I am watching," said the Lord (verse 12). Like a pot about to boil over, His scalding anger was about to be poured out because of the "wickedness" of "my people" (verse 16).

This would be the prophetic theme of the rest of Jeremiah's life; because of the people's stubborn sin and willful forsaking of their God, He was going to use their enemies to punish them. For years Jeremiah warned them with tears that it was coming. But who wants to hear about sinfulness and its unthinkable consequences, especially when there are so many other "prophets of God" who are saying what your itching ears want to hear?

"But what does all this have to do specifically with lament?" you're asking yourself. Jeremiah provides a picture of a people who refuse to repent, to mourn, to lament for their sin. He shows us that all sin must be lamented, or else its painful consequences will become the source for a very different kind of lament. We lament in contrition for our sin or we will lament the suffering that comes because of our sin. Jeremiah and his lamentations provide a powerful picture of the second sort of lament — hopefully to drive us to the first, purposeful form of lament.

REFLECT & DISCUSS:

1. Jeremiah's feelings of inadequacy made him want to reject God's call on his life. In what ways have you shared Jeremiah's response?

2. Jerusalem would be destroyed because of the people's refusal to repent. What is the relationship between repentance and lament?

A CRUEL KING

READ: JEREMIAH 36

Along the way, Jeremiah encountered primarily people who were unwilling to listen to his message. This stubbornness was one of the major sources of his lament. No one was more stubborn than King Jehoiakim. Once again, the purpose of the prophecy was so that "each will turn from his wicked ways" (verse 7).

With the help of his faithful scribe, Baruch, Jeremiah composed a scroll to communicate once again this message of the choice between certain destruction and just as certain forgiveness. Since Jeremiah had been restricted from entering the Temple, Baruch was forced to go there and read the words of warning to the people himself.

When some of the royal officials heard the frightening words of the scroll, they notified the king. "You and Jeremiah, go and hide," (verse 19) they warned, apparently knowing the effect such a scroll would have upon Jehoiakim.

When the scroll finally came into the king's hands, he took out a scribe's pen knife and, cutting the scroll into pieces, threw it into the fire. He would have confronted Jeremiah and Baruch but we are told the Lord had hidden them.

But the story does not end there. The Lord had not hidden them simply for their own protection but so that, after the first scroll had been burned, they could compose another, longer message. Which is exactly what Baruch and Jeremiah did.

Jehoiakim did not want the people to hear the warning words of the scroll (although several already had) and enter into lament for their sin. This is not the first time we have encountered those who stood in the way of lament. David had stubbornly refused to feel the weight of his sin with Bathsheba until the Lord used Nathan to open his eyes and his heart. And Job's friends, who stood in the way of his laments, failed to understand God's intention for them until the end of the story when they were given reason for lamenting their own sinful error in judging and condemning Job, and in the process saying what was not true about the God they thought they knew so well.

The point? See how deeply determined God is that we enter into this dangerous place before the throne. Had Jehoiakim burned a thousand scrolls, we get the impression that God would have had Jeremiah rewrite each one. Had David not listened to Nathan's parable, how many more would the prophet have spoken until the king finally saw the dark truth of what he had done? God is doggedly committed to our coming to Him with our laments of contrition. So committed is He that He sent His only Son to give His life to pay for our sins in order that the response to all such lament will always be the simple, costly word, "Forgiven!"

REFLECT & DISCUSS:

1. Jeremiah 36:3 shows God giving the people yet another chance to turn from their sins by informing them of the consequences if they don't. Sometimes, it is only the fear of penalty that convinces us to "do the right thing." When has this been true in your own life?

2. If you lament your sins based on fear of consequences, does God still listen?

THE COST OF THE CALL

READ: JEREMIAH 37–38; 40:1–6

In two final back-to-back incidents, we see the suffering of Jeremiah because of the call of God on his life. In the first he is arrested, falsely accused, beaten, and thrown into prison. In the second, he is lowered into a muddy cistern.

The suffering inflicted on him, like Job's suffering, is innocent suffering. Jeremiah suffers *because* he is obedient. The source of the suffering could be said to be the call of God on his life. The cause of his suffering is clearly the sin of disbelief of the king and his officials.

After the destruction of Jerusalem, during which Jeremiah was safely in captivity in the courtyard of the guard, he is sought out among the captives by the powerful commander of the imperial guard of Nebuchadnezzar. He, in effect, repeats the core of Jeremiah's prophecy: The Lord had decreed this disaster because of the sin of the people. "But today," he said, "I am freeing you" (40:4).

This section marks the end of the story of Jeremiah, chronologically. As he wandered back to Mizpah, I wonder if that first promise God had made so long ago echoed in his mind, "I am with you and will rescue you" (1:8,19).

A painful life of obedience, characterized by lament, was now coming to an end amidst the smoldering ruins of Jerusalem. Jeremiah had not been saved *from* destruction; he had been saved *through* it.

REFLECT & DISCUSS:

1. Have you ever suffered specifically *because* you were obedient to God's call on your life? How? What was your response to God in this?

2. In Jeremiah 37 and 38, we see that Zedekiah could not decide between public opinion and God's will. When have you struggled with this question in your life? How have you dealt with it?

A NIGHTMARE COME TRUE

READ: JEREMIAH 39; 52

After a siege that lasted over two and a half years, the wall of Jerusalem fell and the Babylonian officials entered the city, taking up the seats of authority in the Middle Gate. Zedekiah fled to the Jordan valley. He was finally apprehended, along with his sons, in the plains of Jericho. His sons were eventually killed in his presence just before his eyes were put out. It was the last horrific image to flash before his mind before it was closed to any more images.

Four thousand six hundred of the survivors were carried off into exile and the holy city burned. The Temple was destroyed and all its valuable metal implements broken up. These two short chapters provide an impassioned, newspaper-type description of the details the book of Lamentations will wail over throughout all of its four dark chapters. These two chapters in Jeremiah provide the factual account we need before we enter into the emotional laments that follow.

If we only possessed the brief facts of the destruction of Jerusalem, it might represent for us only a cipher in the long, painful history of Israel. If we only possessed the description as we have it in Lamentations, we would be tempted to believe that something so horrific could have never really happened.

REFLECT & DISCUSS:

1. What does it tell you about the character of God that He would include in His Word not just the "facts" of history, but long laments about those events?

2. How does it help us to read Jeremiah's laments? Why not just read the historical details and come to our own conclusions?

SPEAKING THE LANGUAGE OF
LAMENT FOR YOURSELF

Jeremiah had plenty of reason to lament. His beloved Jerusalem would come to ruin, his people would suffer unspeakable tragedy, and his own life was painfully short on any sort of joy. His only consolation throughout his life was the Presence of God.

Take some time to think about your own country and your own people: Is there anything there worth lamenting?

Compose a lament based on these thoughts.

THE LAMENTATIONS OF JEREMIAH:
THE VIEW FROM A CAVE

There is a tradition that Lamentations was written by Jeremiah while he was in a cave overlooking Jerusalem. We must imagine ourselves looking over the shoulder of the prophet, past him to an overview of the ruins of Jerusalem. Imagine the smell of smoke and death. Imagine the sounds of weeping and the wailing, especially of the women, the "daughters of Jerusalem" for whom Jeremiah spends so much of his concern and grief.

The unthinkable has happened: Jerusalem, the Holy City, has been destroyed. Jeremiah had repeatedly warned the kings and the people. They had stubbornly refused to listen and repent of their wickedness. In chapters 39 and 52 of Jeremiah, he describes the unthinkable destruction. In giving the Temple over to destruction, God was merely actualizing the truth of what it had become spiritually already, a barren place that the Spirit had already deserted. His curse was merely a pronouncement of the sentence the faithless priests had already passed upon themselves.

Lamentations is the poetry of grief. It is tears reduced to words. It is a Lament of National Disaster, which is still sung in Judaism today. How is Israel supposed to understand the *hesed* of God when it appears that He has become one with her worst enemy? Lamentations pours forth from the wilderness of worship.

As you read through the brief book, see how Lamentations represents an impasse for those who see the world as only black and white, right or wrong. In the course of the passionate outpourings of lament, often things are said that are untrue, God is accused of things of which He is clearly not guilty. The lamenter cries that God does not care or is absent. We know all these could never be true. Lament is a door to another world where a new righteousness is born, based on repentance and not religious correctness.

If we are to move toward a fuller understanding of God, we must embrace some unthinkable paradoxes — for example, that God can appear to become our enemy. His otherness demands it. The result is not the "aha" of understanding, but rather the self-imposed silence of the end of Job. Our silence before Him is seen as the ultimate expression of understanding, but this silence can only come after lament.

Israel stands before the wreckage of the Temple; the disciples stand before the wreckage of the cross. We offer the exhausted poetry of our lament and find the kind of relief that only tears can bring, the kind of silence into which only God can speak. This is the place to which Lamentation leads us.

A LONELY, WEEPING WIDOW

READ: LAMENTATIONS 1

The book opens with a series of portraits of the city as a lonely widow weeping the loss of her beloved (verse 1). She is the queen who has become a slave. She is the virgin daughter whose eyes now overflow with tears because she has been rejected and can find no one to comfort her (verses 2-3).

It is as if Jeremiah must force himself to keep finding examples to say what it is "like" in order to save himself the torture of having to put into words what it actually "is."

Echoing the message of the book of Jeremiah, the only explanation given for the destruction of Jerusalem is her sins (Lamentations 1:8,12). He uses the two awful images in regard to a woman in Judaism: She is naked and she is unclean. At this point Jeremiah begs the Lord to simply "look." His seeing their suffering and humiliation will make all the difference. It is all Jeremiah has left to hope for.

Even now, though it certainly seems too late, Jeremiah pleads with his people to listen. Perhaps it is only now that they finally *can* listen. Perhaps it is only now that they have seen the devastating effect of their sins they will be able to finally lament for them. This is the sad truth of fallenness. Because we will only listen after it is too late, God must Himself act in that too-late moment, because of *hesed,* to save us.

REFLECT *&* DISCUSS:

1. In Lamentations it is clear that Jerusalem has been destroyed because of the sin of the people. How does this compare to the life situation of Job and its message that suffering it not always the result of sin? Do they negate or complement each other?

2. Why is it that a plea for God to simply "look and see" our suffering is such a common theme for lament?

WHEN GOD IS YOUR ENEMY

READ: LAMENTATIONS 2

In the second poem of lament, the absent Groom of chapter 1 is transformed into an angry, pitiless enemy who has "hurled down the splendor" and covered Zion with "the cloud of his anger"(verse 1). The cloud that had always been seen as an element of protection for Israel in the wilderness now represents the most severe threat imaginable: The Lord God of Israel has become their enemy. As the terrifying notion occurs to Jeremiah that God had, in fact, planned all this long ago, he runs out of words. "What can I say for you?" he sobs (verse 13). Jeremiah's eyes have failed. He confesses that his heart has been poured out. But notice that he never says to the people, "I told you so," or "If only you had listened!"

In hopes of arousing God's pity, Jeremiah asks the rhetorical question in verse 20, "Whom have you ever treated like this?" expecting the answer, "No one." But finally, through his tears, Jeremiah sees with startling clarity that this is the "day of the Lord's anger." The only way for his people to respond is to "let [their] tears flow like a river" (verse 18). Through Jeremiah, God had been pleading for His people to lament *for* their sin. Now, after the destruction, all that is left is for them to lament *because* of what their sin has caused.

REFLECT & DISCUSS:

1. What is your response when you realize that God has ordained every bit of tragedy that occurs in this world? How does God want us to respond?

2. Have you ever been in the position of having to lament because of what your sin has caused? How would the situation have been different if you'd repented and lamented sooner?

THE PAIN BECOMES PERSONAL

READ: LAMENTATIONS 3

In chapter 3, the tone of Lamentations shifts as Jeremiah steps from behind the curtain. He begins to speak for himself, in first person. The pain has become personal.

"*I* am the man who has seen affliction!" he laments. "He has driven *me* away!" "He has turned his hands against me!" "He has besieged *me*, surrounded *me*, weighed *me*, walled in *me*!"

Jeremiah has become a "laughingstock." The unrepentant people have made up songs to mock him. This marks his lowest ebb. All Jeremiah's hope in the Lord seems gone.

But then in verse 21, miraculously, a turn happens. Some mystical line is crossed as Jeremiah has exhausted himself against the God who had become his enemy. Having poured all of himself out in lament, he finds in his hopeless emptiness a greater hope than he could have imagined, the hope of *hesed*:

"Because of the LORD's great [*hesed*] we are not consumed" (verse 22).

"His compassions never fail" (verse 22), he sings and one wonders if there is any possibility that he is singing about the same God in chapter 3 that was the source of all his sorrows in chapters 1 and 2. Jeremiah overflows in the kind of overflowing praise that only comes from lament.

"It is good," continues Jeremiah, "to wait quietly for Him," "to hope in Him," "to seek Him" (verse 26).

Still, notice how realistic Jeremiah's new perspective remains. A man still must "bear the yoke," "bury his face in the dust," "offer his cheek to one who would strike him," be "cast off." (verses 27-31) He allows for more suffering in the future, more slaps in the face, more moments of unbearable aloneness. Because of *hesed*, the same God who brings grief will show compassion. (This echoes the hard-bought wisdom of Job 1:21.)

In verse 40 and beyond, Jeremiah proposes a new direction for his people. In a series of "let us" statements, he exhorts the people to let us examine our ways, return to the Lord, lift up our hearts and hands in contrition. In verses 42-47 he provides the lyrics for their lament.

As the lament comes to a close, Jeremiah utilizes the Formula of Remembrance, first to make a list of his own sufferings as a prophet, but then to celebrate God's faithfulness. Hear the repetition, "You heard," "You came," "You said," "You took up," "You have seen" (verses 56-59).

Through the smoke of the rubble, Jeremiah is still able to see the Presence of the Lord. He is able to hold on to Him amidst the confusion by means of lament. He discovers he is able to still praise His faithfulness nevertheless, by means of lament.

Are you able to look through the confusing smoke of the tragedies of your life to see His Presence? More importantly, are you, am I, capable of understanding that our stubborn sin is the cause of most of our sorrows? Sadly, most often it takes the destruction of a city, or of a lifestyle before this kind of clarity comes. And it is through lament that we are able to hold on until the smoke settles and it becomes clear.

REFLECT & DISCUSS:

1. How do you believe Jeremiah would define *hesed*? (See Jeremiah 9:24; 16:5; 31:3,18,31; Lamentations 3:22.)

2. Do you think you would be able to find hope amidst the magnitude of tragedy experienced by Jeremiah? Why or why not?

A SUPREMELY SICKENING VISION
READ: LAMENTATIONS 4 AND 5

In chapter 4, Jeremiah steps back behind the curtain. His eyes have cleared as well, and with a piercing gaze he compares what is now to what once was. The siege of Jerusalem had lasted for two long years. During that time Jeremiah must have witnessed the hopeless horrors of famine that continue today in our otherwise prosperous, well-fed world in places like Sudan. His images of the suffering of the siege are among the most disturbing in the Bible.

Children beg, but no one feeds them.

With a disturbing calmness he coldly calculates that it is better to die by the sword than by famine.

In verse 10, Jeremiah utters what must be the most sickening sentence in all the Bible: "The hands of compassionate women boiled their own children."

The final chapter is an extended plea that the Lord "remember." What follows is a detailed list of what Jeremiah hopes the Lord will not forget: They are now orphans; they are weary; they are bearing the punishment for their father's sins; their women have been ravished; their princes crucified ("hung up by their hands," 5:12). This is the final horrible picture. We leave the people of Judah in their forsaken state.

Lamentations ends with a whimper rather than a bang. It is like the last flickerings of a candle just before its flame sinks into the wax. "Restore us to yourself, O LORD, that we may return; . . . unless you have utterly rejected us and are angry with us beyond measure" (5:21-22).

REFLECT & DISCUSS:

1. What similarities do you see between Jeremiah and David? Between Jeremiah and Job?

2. What was the central characteristic in Jeremiah that allowed him to survive all the turmoil of his life? How was he able to remain faithful?

SPEAKING THE LANGUAGE OF LAMENT FOR YOURSELF

We've looked at the laments of Job, David, and Jeremiah. We've not yet reached the place where Jesus arrives to change everything — to bring the ultimate hope to a dark, hurting world.

Imagine what it would be like if you didn't know Christ. What shape would your laments take?

Compose a lament based on that thought.

JESUS

ALL THINGS COME TOGETHER

As we leave Jeremiah, alone in his cave overlooking what is left of Jerusalem, the road makes a sharp uphill turn. It steeply rises to a saddle, overlooking the city. A small crowd is gathered there, pilgrims perhaps for one of the *shelosh relagim* (the three great feasts). A quick scan of the crowd reveals no one out of the ordinary. They are all simple Jewish faces. But it seems everyone is deferring to one average-looking man. He is young and slightly built, His eyes so dark that you cannot make out a pupil. He does not stand out until you take a moment to linger on His face. Though He is visibly tired, He seems to be listening as much as He is listened to. He cannot speak to someone, it seems, unless He has a hand resting on one of their shoulders. He does not respond until they stop and look Him in the face. It is, of course, *Jeshua ben Josef.* Jesus, the Nazarene.

He looks up in our direction as we approach. Without our having to tell Him, He already knows the difficult journey we've been on. The sympathetic look on His face says it all. After all, He set His foot on this same path long centuries before we were born. Above everyone else we've met along this road, He seems the most anxious to join us.

Paul said, in Colossians 1:17, that in Jesus "all things hold together." One thing he is referring to is *truth*. Everything that is true comes together in the life of Jesus of Nazareth, who called Himself the Truth. The various truths we've seen scattered through the Old Testament, over centuries of time, through the lives of men like Job, David, and Jeremiah, all those truths come together and find meaningful unity (they "hold together") only in Jesus Christ, this ordinary Galilean craftsman.

The truth about Presence finds its fulfillment and meaning in the Incarnation. The untranslatable word *hesed* begins to make perfect sense as the life of Jesus "holds together" all its various meanings. In His life, its meaning comes alive. The line we saw so many lamenters cross (*vav* adversative) was finally drawn in the sand of Golgotha. Most especially, of all the tears we saw, of all the laments we heard, the tears and laments of Jesus held together all the sorrows and grief, offering them to the Father in one perfect sacrifice. The laments of the ages called Him forth. The long lament we know as *Maranatha*, will call Him back someday.

Seven centuries before Jesus was born, Isaiah was given to see that His life would be defined by sorrow. Men would reject Him, as indeed they did and continue all over the world to do. He would be a man of sorrows who, through His incarnation, would become familiar with our suffering. That surely would have been enough, but Isaiah surprises us with the good news that He would take up those sorrows and carry, on His own feeble frame, our infirmities. A life defined by lament.

And now, at last, He has come to join us for the remainder of our journey. After a few moments we might begin to wonder how we ever got along without Him, but in truth He has been with us every stumbling step of the way.

HESED INFLESHED

READ: JOHN 1:1-14

When we cross over from the Old Testament to the New, we also make the jump from the language of Hebrew to Greek. Though the language has changed, the thought patterns largely remain the same. We must try to detect the Hebrew thought as it is reflected in the language of Greek.

In the first chapter of the gospel of John, we read that the "Word became flesh." The Greek word for "word" is *logos* and so most of the commentaries have followed the trail of Greek philosophical thought, because John was writing to a largely Greek-speaking Gentile audience. Of course John would attempt to connect with their way of thought. When he is forced to use a Hebrew word, such as *Rabbi* (John 1:38) or *Messiah* (1:41) or a place name such as the "Sea of Galilee" (6:1), John almost always translates it for his Greek audience. But he thinks as a thoroughly Jewish man.

I would like to suggest (and people much smarter than I have already disagreed with this idea!) that when John uses the word *Word*, he has in mind Old Testament passages such as Psalms 33:6 and 136:5, where the *word* of the Lord was the creative force through which God made the universe. This also seems to be reflected in John 1:3, "Through him all things were made; without him nothing was made that has been made."

Psalm 136 also celebrates the *hesed* of God. One of the closest Greek parallels to the Hebrew word *hesed* is "grace." John affirms in 1:14,16 and elsewhere that Jesus is "Full of grace." The *New Living Translation* goes so far as to translate this word "unfailing love," an even closer parallel to *hesed*.

Could it be that the "Word" that became flesh was actually *hesed*? *God's hesed became flesh in Jesus Christ.*

We will see that much of Jesus' ministry and many of His parables were really an attempt to define this indefinable word. Most powerfully, however, He perfectly translated it by means of his singularly perfect life. He defined the defining characteristic of God — *hesed* — in the only way it could be defined: He incarnated it.

REFLECT & DISCUSS:

1. In what ways does Jesus define the word *hesed*?

2. What does it tell you about God's character that He sent us a living, breathing example of His *hesed*? What does it tell you about His desires for us?

ENEMY LOVE

READ: LUKE 6:27-36

Another way *hesed* can be translated is "enemy love" (see Proverbs 25:21). When David realized that he had become the enemy of God because of his sin with Bathsheba, it was to God's *hesed* that he appealed (see Psalm 51:1). In the face of our own enemies, Jesus demands that we demonstrate this surprising mercy.

In Luke 6:32-34, Jesus speaks of the expectations that come from the original equation. You love people who deserve it; you do good to others because they've done good to you, and so on. This perfectly matches the mentality of Satan's accusation of Job to God (see Job 1:9). Jesus calls into question the old notion, making way for a totally new and unexpected mercy. He is completing the equation we saw in the book of Job.

In Luke 6:35, Jesus' conclusion could be a textbook definition of the word *hesed*. "He [God] is kind to the ungrateful and wicked." In this light I wonder if the next verse, 36, might well be translated, "Do *hesed*, just as your Father does *hesed*."

Hesed incarnate. *Hesed* powerfully preached and lived out. And finally, *hesed* demanded of His followers.

REFLECT & DISCUSS:

1. Read the parables of the Good Samaritan (Luke 10:25-37), the Prodigal Son (Luke 15:11-32), and the Workers (Matthew 20:1-16). How can we better understand *hesed* from these passages?

2. How is it possible to "do *hesed*"? List several ways you could do this in your life.

ANOTHER WEEPING PROPHET

READ: LUKE 13:34-35; 19:41-44

At least once Jesus was mistaken for Jeremiah, the "weeping prophet" (see Matthew 16:13-14). We do not know if this was because He had been seen openly weeping or that He had echoed Jeremiah's prophecy and predicted yet another destruction of Jerusalem. Perhaps people sensed in Jesus that something had indeed "come together" as it had in Jeremiah, who was, like Jesus, both prophet and priest.

In Luke 13:34, Jesus is only three days away from entering Jerusalem for the last time. He has just received a warning from the Pharisees to flee Herod. Jesus responds to their cautioning by issuing a warning of His own. He insists He will continue on with His ministry of healing and casting out demons for two more days. On the third day, Jesus says, He will arrive in Jerusalem.

In verses 34-35, Jesus laments for the city. He speaks of the desire of His heart to gather the children together. While He describes Herod as a fox, Jesus likens His desire to that of a mother hen, gathering her chicks under the shelter of her wings. Echoing the words of Jeremiah 22:5, He pronounces that the house is desolate. Loving compassion and shelter were offered, but the people rejected them.

Luke 19:41 occurs just three days later. Jesus is making His so-called "triumphal entry" into Jerusalem. He is riding the colt, a sign that He was coming in peace. The Passover crowd has pressed in around Him and some are actually pronouncing that very blessing from Psalm 118. Others are ironically making the same pronouncement the angels had made when He was born, "Peace in heaven and glory in the highest." (19:38)

Luke tells us in verse 41 that when Jesus saw the city He began to openly weep. "If only" provides the forsaken tone of the lament. If only they had known. If only they had seen. But it has been hidden from their eyes. Jesus prophetically sees the destruction of the city that will occur in less than forty years. He sees the siege ramp that Titus will build. He sees, as Jeremiah saw, the suffering of the children. Jesus sees it all, every detail. He bursts into tears.

All because they had not recognized the time of God's coming to them. That very moment, when the Presence of God came riding a smelly foal. When the Incarnation of *Hesed*, God's defining characteristic, came weeping, uncontrollably like a little boy. Like Jeremiah, the tears of men and God mingled in Jesus' eyes, only with infinitely greater depth.

REFLECT *&* DISCUSS:

1. What prompted Jesus to lament in Luke 13:34? What was the theme of this lament?

2. What is the major difference between Jesus' and Jeremiah's laments over Jerusalem?

3. Jesus laments because He sees the future of Jerusalem. Can you think of a time when you lamented your own future because of the consequences of your past behavior?

LAMENT AND THE MEAL

READ: LUKE 22:14-38; JOHN 13

When Jesus shares the final meal with His disciples, He tells them how eagerly He desired to spend this time together with them. Meal fellowship in Jesus' day carried with it a sense of deep intimacy, even healing. This meal, above all others, would provide an invitation to us all to share intimately with Jesus and to draw near and be healed through it.

Luke gives us more detail than the other gospels. Only he provides the vital discourse on servanthood, without which we might fail to see the bridge over to John 13 and the washing of the disciples' feet.

Seeing all that lay ahead of Him in His mind, Jesus takes the cup and the bread, telling them this is His blood and flesh. The disciples will erupt into an argument about who is the greatest. Jesus will fall on His knees and wash their feet, including even Judas' feet.

He will predict His death. He will prophesy that they will desert Him, that one will betray and another deny. He will warn Peter that, like Job, Satan has asked to sift him like wheat. So Peter learns of the throne room scene of which Job was so tragically ignorant. But it will make no difference in Peter's denial.

The impact and the price of sin, remembered in the Passover meal, was about to become infinitely magnified in Jesus' life and experience. His tears would fall on account of our sin. His blood would be poured out so that it could mark the door posts of our hearts.

Mark tells us they sang a hymn and left. The tradition was to sing the second half of the *Hallel* or "Hallelujah" psalms (113-118). But given the confusion, the talk of death and betrayal, given that in a few moments Jesus would speak of His soul being "overwhelmed with sorrow to the point of death" (Mark 14:34), it is not hard to imagine that even their hallelujahs sounded more like a lament.

REFLECT & DISCUSS:

1. In Luke 22:19, Jesus says to the disciples (and us), "This is my body given for you." Knowing what you know now, what type of response might be appropriate when you hear those words spoken during Communion?

2. The Lord's Supper is an invitation for us to draw near to Jesus. What might you appropriately lament during this time?

SPEAKING THE LANGUAGE OF
LAMENT FOR YOURSELF

Like Job, Jeremiah, and David before Him, Jesus lamented the peoples' sin,
their separation from God, and the falleness of the world. Take a moment to
reflect on the laments of Jesus. Then compose a lament of your own.

JESUS

THE MAN OF SORROWS

We turn around for a moment and He is gone. And for a while it seems that we are once again traveling on this pathway of lament all alone. But up ahead we hear a commotion and as we draw near, we see the excruciating sight of three men hanging from wooden crosses.

The two on either side are doing the macabre crucifixion "dance," pushing up on a nail driven through their ankles, gasping a breath until they can bear the pain no more, then finally falling back onto the nails that are fixed through their wrists. Up and down they dance and shout and curse, focusing their venom on the blood-covered victim hanging between them.

He too is "dancing." He pushes up to grab a breath and utters one of several short gasping phrases. But He is not shouting. He is forgiving. He is providing a home for His mother. He is praying.

If we fail to understand this moment of lament, we will never understand all that lament can mean. At the moment when Jesus was being most used by God, He was lamenting. By the looks of it, this would seem to be the end of our road of lament. In fact, Jesus tells us, it is just the beginning.

CROSSING THE LINE IN THE GARDEN

READ: LUKE 22:39-46

The blood bath began in the garden. He was a bloody mess before anyone even laid a hand on Him. Luke tells us they went out as usual to the Mount of Olives. On the mount was a privately owned garden called "Gethsemane," which means "place of crushing," because there was an olive press located there. When they arrived Jesus began to feel the crushing weight of His own fear and sorrow.

Jesus moves away and kneels. He makes the sort of disturbingly honest statement to the Father that we have become used to hearing in lament. "If there is any way to get me out of this, I want out." He knows that the Father's will is for Him to die a torturous death. In the openness of lament He responds, "I don't want this!" Was He supposed to keep silent about all this before the Father?

Matthew tells us He prayed this over three periods of time. An angel, we are told, appeared to encourage Him, but apparently it was to no avail. His anguish peaks. His sweat becomes blood. He wins the battle with the words, "Not what I want, but what You want." The line we have seen in so many laments, from "me" to "You," was crossed once and for all.

Could it be that the same throne-room scene was taking place that we saw in Job? Was the Accuser snarling that Jesus had only lived the perfect life He lived because something was in it for Him? Now the time had come to make the exchange Job had made, only on an infinitely larger scale: to give up everything in order to receive everything. Only for Jesus, the "everything" was not for Himself, but for you and me.

REFLECT & DISCUSS:

1. Have you ever begged God to let you out of something you knew you were supposed to do? How did that conversation go? Did you cross the line from "me" to "you," or try to hang on to your own will?

2. Does the prophetic title, "Man of Sorrows," imply that this is all Jesus' life is about? Does the presence of sorrow preclude the presence of any joy or is the experience of the depth and reality of sorrow the necessary condition for real joy?

THE GOD-FORSAKEN GOD

READ: MATTHEW 27:45-46

If all lament is related to Presence, then Jesus' experience of the absence of God, for the only time in all eternity, must be the focal point of all lament.

If the answer to lament always has to do with *hesed,* then Jesus forgiving His enemies from the cross (including you and me) — is the ultimate expression of *hesed* — "enemy love."

If Job begins the lesson on innocent suffering, Jesus on the cross brings it to complete perfection. If Jeremiah weeps for the people and for God, then it is only through the tears of Jesus on the cross that God and the people will be brought together once more. If lament helps to give meaningful language to suffering, then Jesus on the cross shows us how God uses suffering to save the world.

Read those two short verses and allow them to speak to the heart of your imagination. Any hurt you've ever felt is there. Every sin you've ever committed is there. Every fear, every moment of loneliness, every pang of betrayal. It is all there. It all comes together, is held together, long enough for them to exhaust themselves against God.

REFLECT & DISCUSS:

1. Is Incarnation the only hope for defining an untranslatable word? What other difficult ideas were brought to perfect clarity in the incarnation of Jesus?

2. Why did Jesus say the Father had forsaken Him? Could such a thing be possible?

JOB'S VISION REALIZED

Though you might open your Bible and find them in the book of Job, I'll provide them for you again here: the three sublime visions in which Job saw Jesus. Note that each of these statements was part prophecy, part lament. Job's heart cried out for an arbitrator, an advocate, a friend, and a redeemer. Each of these laments finds its answer in Jesus.

> If only there were someone to arbitrate between us,
>> to lay his hand upon us both,
>>> someone to remove God's rod from me,
>> so that his terror would frighten me no more. (Job 9:33-34)

Through the spectacles of his suffering, Job saw that Someone else was needed to remove the rod of God's wrath from him. In Romans 5:9, Paul exclaims, "Since we have now been justified by his blood, how much more shall we be saved from God's wrath through him!"

> Even now my witness is in heaven;
>> my *Advocate* is on high.
> My intercessor is my *Friend*
>> as my eyes pour out tears to God;
>> on behalf of a man he pleads with God
> as a man pleads for his friend. (Job 16:19-21, emphasis added)

John confirms that Jesus speaks to the Father in our defense, saying, "We have an Advocate with the Father, Jesus Christ the righteous" (1 John 2:1, JPS). Job saw this Intercessor was also a friend — a revolutionary and unlikely concept, especially in Job's day. But Jesus Himself would later call us His friends (see John 15:15).

> I know that my *Redeemer* lives,
>> and that in the end he will stand upon the earth.
>> And after my skin has been destroyed,
>> yet in my flesh I will see God;
>>> myself will see him
>> with my own eyes—I, and not another.

How my heart yearns within me! (Job 19:25-27, emphasis added)

In Galatians 3:13, Paul reiterates Christ's role as Redeemer, saying that He has redeemed us from the curse of the law by being made a curse for us. In Job's darkest time of lament, in his deepest moment of need, he called out for an advocate, friend, and redeemer — and saw Jesus.

REFLECT & DISCUSS:

1. Job cried out that his "heart yearned" within him. What about your heart? For what do you yearn? What brings on these longings?

2. Job's laments led him to envision the Savior. How would this have been possible, because no one had told Him of Christ's coming?

3. Our laments might not naturally lead us to Jesus. They could easily lead us back to ourselves, or down a path of looking for someone to blame for the trials in our lives. Where do your laments lead you? How can we be sure lament will take us in the "right" direction?

THE VOICE OF DAVID'S LAMENT

Job was not the only one of our lamenters whose words foreshadowed the coming of Jesus and His death on the cross for us. The darkness that covered the land during the Crucifixion was the same darkness that David had lamented in Psalm 18. When Jesus cried out in one of His last short, gasping phrases from the cross, it was in the words of David's lament in the opening verse of Psalm 22.

The laments contain the most detailed descriptions of the Crucifixion. Both Zechariah and Jeremiah had seen the price of the thirty pieces of silver (see Zechariah 11:12; Jeremiah 32:6-9). Psalm 22:18 predicts the soldiers gambling for Jesus' coat. Psalm 69:21 speaks of the vinegar He was given to drink. Psalm 109:25 tells of the mocking of the crowd.

But Psalm 22:16 contains the real treasure. It says, "They have pierced my hands and my feet."

Look as long as you like at the Gospel accounts of the Crucifixion and you will not find this detail. The only hint we have is Jesus pointing out the nail prints after the Resurrection first to the disciples (see John 20:20) and then later to Thomas (see 20:24-27).

Even as Job saw Jesus more clearly than had anyone before, so David, who had suffered so much in his life, was granted a vision clearer even than most of Jesus' contemporaries. Through lament they had miraculously entered into the "fellowship of sharing in his sufferings" (Philippians 3:10).

REFLECT & DISCUSS:

1. On the cross, is Jesus quoting David's psalm (22) or was David prophetically quoting Jesus? Does this distinction really matter?

2. The prophets entered into fellowship with Jesus through suffering and lament. Is that the only path to a true relationship with Christ? Are there others? If we hold back our laments, is it possible to be in true fellowship with Jesus?

SPEAKING THE LANGUAGE OF LAMENT FOR YOURSELF

Now, spend some time entering into the lament of Jesus on the cross. In a very real sense His lament is yours and mine. We inflicted the suffering ourselves on Him. He cries out to the Father on our behalf as well, "Forgive them, for they do not know what they are doing"(Luke 23:34).

Now is the time to see, as Job saw through lament, that the sorrow we carry for our sin must become our vital connection with Him.

> He was despised and rejected by men,
>   a man of sorrows, and familiar with suffering. . . .
> Surely he took up our infirmities
>   and carried our sorrows. (Isaiah 53:3-4)

Ask God to reveal your sin to you, so that you might lament and confess. Feel your sorrow, and meditate on the fact that Jesus has taken that sorrow and offered His life on the cross in exchange. Spend some time journaling your laments.

CONCLUSIONS

We have been on a long journey together, this journey of lament. We have learned so much, thanks to the biblical companions who have joined us along the way and traveled awhile with us. "Nearing Home" is really a misnomer, because the Word is clear, this world is not our home (see 1 Peter 1:17). Since the Fall and the beginning of lament in the garden, it could never again be home.

What the language of lament would have us understand is that this pathway, this journey, is in fact the only true home we will ever know here. It is not comfortable but it is *real*. It is not secure but it is *true*. In a world of untruth and illusion, finding our home in the middle of this path is all that matters. It is the place we belong because it is the place where we encounter Him. How can we say we follow the Man of Sorrows when we are so unfamiliar with this path of grief?

THE KEY TO RENEWED PRESENCE

READ: GENESIS 3

As we saw, lament had a precise beginning in the garden. It came about when Adam and Eve doubted the *hesed* of God, when they disbelieved His word to them concerning the tree of good and evil.

As a result of their disbelieving doubt, the first couple went into hiding. They did not want their Creator to see their glorious nakedness, which now to them appeared so shameful. Their view of the world, of themselves, and of the Father has become twisted and out of focus. Eating from the fruit of the knowledge of good and evil had resulted in their fundamental misunderstanding of it. They felt foolish and embarrassingly uncovered. What else was there to do, except hide?

The key to unlocking the issue of Presence, so fundamental in our understanding of lament, is provided in the exchange that begins in Genesis 3:8. Aware of their disobedience, it is the Lord who first calls out to the hidden couple. He seeks. They hide. He pursues. They flee. "Where are you?" (verse 9). His kind voice echoes among the perfect trees.

"I heard the sound of Your voice in the garden and I was afraid, so I hid," Adam whines from behind a bush.

The beginning of the sad separation is evident in Adam's voice. What matters most for our discussion is that he was the one who went into hiding. His sin became fear, and the fear drove him and his luminous partner from the Presence.

You and I cower behind the same sort of undergrowth. Something deep in us fears and runs and hides and then sits behind the bush and wonders when God will come and find us. The glorious truth is that, because of *hesed,* He is always on the way. Though we will never deserve such loving attention, He is the good Shepherd, looking for the foolish sheep until He finds us. Lament is nothing more than the bleating of the lost ones.

In the garden the first human tears fell. The first couple went into hiding and the God of *hesed* began His pursuit.

REFLECT & DISCUSS:

1. What is your initial reaction to the picture of God lovingly, persistently pursuing His lost sheep?

2. After the journey you've been on, how do you view your connection with that beginning? Is it merely a "Bible tale" or is it a point of contact for your own experience of lament?

3. When you sense the absence of His Presence what happens when you simply "turn around"? Have you ever had this experience?

THE SWEET SCROLL

READ: EZEKIEL 2:9–3:3

Then I looked, and I saw a hand stretched out to me. In it was
a scroll, which he unrolled before me. On both sides of it were
written words of lament and mourning and woe.

And he said to me, "Son of man, eat what is before you, eat
this scroll; then go and speak to the house of Israel." So I opened
my mouth, and he gave me the scroll to eat.

Then he said to me, "Son of man, eat this scroll I am giving
you and fill your stomach with it." So I ate it, and it tasted as sweet
as honey in my mouth. (Ezekiel 2:9–3:3)

Now that you have traveled the pathway of lament, I hope Ezekiel's experience
no longer surprises you. When God presented the scroll to Ezekiel, His
desire was to teach the people of Israel the vocabulary of repentance. But
they were unwilling to speak it and the consequences were dire — a warning
for us of what always follows when we stubbornly say "no" when God offers
us the scroll of lament.

We all hold such a scroll in our hands, the Word of God, which we have
seen is so full of lament. Today, He invites us to taste and see that what we
imagined as bitter and foul tasting will lead us to a sweetness we could have
never expected.

REFLECT & DISCUSS:

1. Why do we — along with the people of Israel — imagine lament as
   bitter and foul tasting? Why do we reject it? Why are the consequences
   so dire when we reject it?

2. How is it possible that lament could taste "as sweet as honey" in your
   mouth? What changes it from bitter and foul to "sweet"? Have you
   experienced this change?

LAMENTING THE THORNS

To keep me from becoming conceited because of these surpassingly great revelations, there was given me a thorn in my flesh, a messenger of Satan, to torment me. Three times I pleaded with the Lord to take it away from me. But he said to me, "My grace is sufficient for you, for my power is made perfect in weakness." Therefore I will boast all the more gladly about my weaknesses, so that Christ's power may rest on me. That is why, for Christ's sake, I delight in weaknesses, in insults, in hardships, in persecutions, in difficulties. For when I am weak, then I am strong.

2 CORINTHIANS 12:7-10

Paul's struggle with the mysterious thorn shines a light on lament from a slightly different angle. God had revealed Himself to Paul in "surpassingly great revelations." But the apostle had become conceited about his new knowledge. And so a "messenger of Satan" arrived. Could its coming have been the result of the same sort of throne-room scene we saw in the book of Job?

When Paul pleaded that the pain go away, God answered "no." And then comes the ray of new light. "My grace (*hesed?*) is enough for you because my power is made perfect through your weakness" (my translation).

Hearing this, Paul crosses the line from his own preoccupation with his pain to a new place before the throne, from "me" to "You." When he is weak then, in effect, God is seen in a new and powerful way. From this point on, Paul chose weakness.

Lament is a part of that deliberate choice to embrace the new meaning found in pain and weakness. It understands that only after such submission will a new strength be born.

REFLECT *&* DISCUSS:

1. Have you ever become "conceited" in your knowledge of Christ, the Bible, or Christianity in general? What happened? How can you avoid this conceit?

2. What are some of your thorns? Have you lamented them? How might you receive strength from them?

THE END OF LAMENT

For the Lamb at the center of the throne will be their shepherd;
     he will lead them to springs of living water.
     And God will wipe away every tear from their eyes.

REVELATION 7:17

And I heard a loud voice from the throne saying, "Now the dwelling of God is with men, and he will live with them. They will be his people, and God himself will be with them and be their God. He will wipe every tear from their eyes. There will be no more death or mourning or crying or pain, for the old order of things has passed away."

     He who was seated on the throne said, "I am making everything new!"

REVELATION 21:3-5

In order to help us bear the burden, the Lord gives lament. But there is another gift He gives to make the journey bearable. It is a gift He chose not to give His servant Job. It is a vision into the throne room of God.

John is the communicator of this "unveiling." He explains in Revelation that there is an end of lament in all our futures. He himself has seen it!

John first sees the Lamb, who is also the seeking Shepherd we have been talking so much about. There, before the throne, John hears that this One who is also known as the "Man of Sorrows" will someday wipe away their tears. The word for "wipe away" is better translated "wipe out!" The image is not of a tender Kleenex moment but more a matter of the wiping out of tears for all time.

The second vision involves a renewal of the Presence of God that was first broken in the garden. From now on, He Himself will be with them. The effect of the immediacy of His Presence? No more death or pain; no more tears!

This promised vision, though not realized yet, is still in effect. John has seen it — in the heavenlies it has already happened!

This confidence informs our laments, yours and mine, today. This is precisely what Paul meant when he said we do not grieve (lament) as those who have no hope (see 1 Thessalonians 4:13). The Man of Sorrows, who was so familiar with suffering, who wept our tears on the cross, is the same One who will wipe out tears for good one day. He is our Hope.

REFLECT & DISCUSS:

1. What do you make of the fact that in Revelation we still hear lament? (See Revelation 6:9.) Do you hear the promise in 21:4 as the end of all lament?

2. What is the difference between grieving as those "who have no hope," and biblical lament?

LOOKING BACK TO SEE
HOW FAR WE'VE COME

Return to the first week and ask yourself the same questions once more. Write your answers, and compose a lament based on them.

1. What is God worth?

2. When does God seem closest to you?

3. What does God's *hesed* mean to you?

4. What has God done in your life that's worth remembering?

5. When have you "crossed the line" from lament to praise in your prayers?

ANNOTATED BIBLIOGRAPHY

✤

Allender, Dan. *The Hidden Hope in Lament*. Bainbridge Island, WA :
Mars Hill Review 1 pgs 25-38. 1994. Early on, when I first began
researching lament, someone sent me this wonderful article. I was a bit
disappointed to read several ideas in this article that I thought I had
thought of! This is the best brief introduction to the major themes of
lament.

Berrigan, Daniel. *Lamentations: From New York to Kabul and Beyond*. Chicago:
Sheed and Ward, Chicago, 2002. Brennan Manning put this book
into my hands one day as we were browsing the shelves of the local
bookstore. Berrigan's radical voice has been a truly prophetic one for
our times. In this book he seeks to bring to the events of 9-11 into focus
through the lens of Lamentations.

Brener, Anne. *Mourning and Mitzvah: A Guided Journal for Walking the Mourner's
Path Through Grief to Healing*. Woodstock: Jewish Lights, 1997. The
best introduction to Jewish mourning customs known to me. Perhaps
without knowing it, Brener has also written a practical primer on
lament.

Brueggemann, Walter. *The Psalms: The Life of Faith*. Minneapolis: Fortress
Press, 1995. This is the single most important book on lament you will
ever read. Brueggemann has digested for us all the academic work that
has been done on the psalms and provided categories for us to approach
and understand the psalms for ourselves. He does not tell us what
to think about the psalms. He teaches us how to think about them.
Besides being first rate scholarship, this book is beautifully written.

Brueggemann, Walter. *The Message of the Psalms*. Minneapolis: Augsburg,
1984. This is a more concentrated presentation of Brueggemann's
three-fold approach to the psalms; a. psalms of orientation, b. psalms of
disorientation (laments) and c. psalms of a new orientation.

Brueggemann, Walter. *The Threat of Life: Sermons on Pain, Power, and Weakness.* Minneapolis: Fortress, 1996. This is a collection of sermons, primarily from the Old Testament. They are a striking testimony to the dangerous prospect of what can happen when the Bible is truly opened.

Brueggemann, Walter. *Awed to Heaven, Rooted in Earth: Prayers of Walter Brueggemann.* Minneapolis: Fortress, 2003. For forty-two years Brueggemann opened his Old Testament classes with a prayer that he had composed beforehand that focused on the text of the day. They are both beautiful in their language and deeply troubling in their degree of intimacy. There are several examples of modern-day lament in this book.

Carson, D.A. *Holy Sonnets of the Twentieth Century.* Grand Rapids: Baker, 1994. Our finest New Testament scholar is also one of our finest hymn writers. You will find in several of them Carson's deep personal understanding of lament.

Clark, Gordon R. "The Word Hesed in the Hebrew Bible," *Journal for the Study of the Old Testament* Supplement Series 157, Sheffield, 1993. You'll never find this one in your local bookstore! It is an extremely technical linguistic approach to *hesed* based on what Clark calls the "lexical field" approach. Still, if you get serious about understanding this word you need to work through this book.

Crabb, Larry. *Shattered Dreams: God's Unexpected Pathway to Joy.* Colorado Springs: Waterbrook, 2001. Without actually using the word, this penetrating book provides the finest foundation for understanding our need to lament. Shattered dreams are where all lament comes from.

Floysvik, Ingvar. *When God Becomes My Enemy: The Theology of the Complaint Psalms.* St. Louis: Concordia Academic Press, 1997. This book focuses on interpreting five representative imprecatory psalms (6, 44, 74, 88, and 90). Though it was presented originally as a dissertation, this book is the most intellectually honest work known to me on the psalms of imprecation. Floysvik is also a wonderful writer.

Gerstenberger, Erhard S. "Psalms, Part 2 and Lamentations," Volume XV, *The Forms of Old Testament Literature*. Grand Rapids: Eerdmanns, 2001. This is an exhaustive form-critical analysis of Psalms and Lamentations. It represents the finest work in form criticism on the subject.

Heater, Homer. "Structure and Meaning in Lamentations." BSac 149:595 (Jul 92), p. 305. A good article on the different acrostic structures in Lamentations.

Henderson, Frank. *Liturgies of Lament*. Chicago: Liturgy Training Publications, 1994. It was this fine book that introduced me to the notion of "themed services of lament." A fine resource for any pastor who wants to move his people in the direction of corporate lament.

Hsu, Albert Y. *Grieving a Suicide: A Loved One's Search for Comfort, Answers and Hope*. Downers Grove: InterVarsity Press, 2002. Al is a good friend who not only endured his father's suicide but processed the pain in as redemptive a way as I have ever seen. The book, perhaps without realizing it, provides a basis for understanding the emotional benefits of lament.

Jinkins, Michael. *In the House of the Lord: Inhabiting the Psalms of Lament*. Collegeville, Minn.: The Liturgical Press, 1998. This book is in my top two favorites on lament. Though Jinkins is a scholar, he also possesses a pastor's heart which processes all the academic material for us by means of a pastoral imagination. His concern for liturgy and practical application reveal this sensitivity. He, like Brueggemann, is a superb writer. I found the phrase "God-forsaken God" in this book.

Kidner, Derek. *Psalms: An Introduction and Commentary*. Downers Grove: Inter-Varsity Press, 1973. Finest basic commentary on the psalms I know. Kidner reveals a profound understanding of lament as well.

Leithart, Peter J. *From Silence to Song: The Davidic Liturgical Revolution*. Moscow, ID: Canon Press, Moscow, 2003. A compelling presentation of the impact of David on Israel's worship, particularly in his reorganization of the tabernacle.

Lewis, C.S. *A Grief Observed.* New York: Bantam, 1980. Lewis' own lament journal on the death of his wife, Joy. A compelling portrait of honest grief and the process of lament.

Moore, R. Kelvin. *The Psalms of Lamentation and the Enigma of Suffering,* Volume 50. Lewiston: Mellen Biblical Press, 1996. This is another book you will have difficulty finding. It looks at the reasons, reactions, and resolutions of suffering in the lament psalms.

Peterson, Eugene. *Leap Over a Wall.* San Francisco: Harper, 1997. Without a doubt, the best book on the emotional life of David there is. It provides a profound understanding of the heart of David through the various struggles of his life and kingship. Read this first and then work through the psalms of David and you will never be the same.

Sakenfeld, Katherine Doob. *The Meaning of* Hesed *in the Hebrew Bible: A New Inquiry.* Eugene: Wipf and Stock, 1978. This is one of the most important books on *hesed.* It seeks to unpack its range of meaning from sacred and secular pre-exilic prose. Most helpful to me were the last two chapters on *hesed* in the prophets and in the Wisdom literature. This is another dissertation that proved so important that it was published in book form.

Seerveld, Calvin. "Reading and Hearing the Psalms: The Gut of the Bible," *Pro Rege:* 27:4 (June 1999), pp. 20-32.

"Pain Is a Four-Letter Word: A Congregational Lament," *Reformed Worship:* 72 (June 2004), pp. 6-7. Calvin, who got me into this lament mess in the first place, e-mailed these wonderful articles on lament. The first provides a superb basis for understanding the emotionality of the psalms. The second is an explanation for one of his own hymns, "A Congregational Lament." While reading the second article, I realized that when he challenged me all those years ago after 9-11 to wrestle with biblical lament, it was a journey he himself had been on for quite some time. I am thankful that, instead of spoon feeding me answers, he issued a challenge to come onto the dance floor on my own. That is the mark of a true mentor.

Tileston, Mary W. editor "Great Souls at Prayer." Cambridge: James Clarke and Co, 1898. An historical collection which contains several prayers of lament.

Westermann, Claus. *Praise and Lament in the Psalms*. Atlanta: John Knox Press, 1981.

"*Lamentations: Issues and Interpretation*. Minneapolis: Fortress, 1994. Westermann was the first academic in our time to wrestle with the psalms of lament at the level of the imagination. These are some of the most excellent examples of biblical scholarship you will ever find.

Wiesel, Elie. *Five Biblical Portraits: Saul, Jonah, Jeremiah, Elijah and Joshua*. Notre Dame: University of Notre Dame Press, 1981. Who better to help us understand lament in the lives of these different biblical characters than Wiesel, himself a survivor of the holocaust? These books are also excellent introductions to rabbinic thought.

Wipf, Jane Larson. *A Fistful of Agates*. New York: Vantage, 2004. This is one of the finest journals of lament known to me. God used this powerful book to introduce me at an emotional level to what lament is all about.

Zuck, Roy B. editor. *Sitting With Job: Selected Studies on the Book of Job*. Grand Rapids: Baker, 1992. This is a superb collection of essays on various topics from the book of Job. In my opinion one of the most important is Matitiahu Tsevat's, "The Meaning of the Book of Job." It was this essay which introduced me to the notion that Job contains far more than simply a discussion of the question of theodicy.

Author

MICHAEL CARD is an award-winning musician, author, and teacher. His many songs include "El Shaddai" and "Immanuel." He has also written numerous books, including *A Violent Grace*, *The Parable of Joy*, and *A Fragile Stone*. A graduate of Western Kentucky University with a bachelor's and master's degree in biblical studies, Card is currently at work on a Ph.D. in classical literature. Michael lives in Tennessee with his wife and four children.

For more materials, Bible study read-through notes, and other audio resources, discussions, and recorded musical laments, go to www.michaelcard.com.

More from Michael Card.

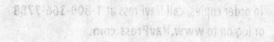

SUPPORT THE MINISTRY OF THE NAVIGATORS

The Navigators' calling is to advance the Gospel of Jesus and His Kingdom into the nations through spiritual generations of laborers living and discipling among the lost.

Navigators have invested their lives in people for more than 75 years, coming alongside them life-on-life to help them passionately know Christ and to make Him known.

The U.S. Navigators' ministry touches lives in varied settings, including college campuses, military bases, downtown offices, urban neighborhoods, prisons, and youth camps.

Dedicated to helping people navigate spiritually, The Navigators aim to make a permanent difference in the lives of people around the world. The Navigators help their communities of friends to follow Christ passionately and equip them effectively to go out and do the same.

To learn more about donating to The Navigators' ministry,
go to **www.navigators.org/us/support**
or call toll-free at **1-866-568-7827**.